4/19/2024

TRANSCENDED

Story of an African Science Professor

Changing Lives in America

Dr. Steve Opoku-Duah

ISBN 978-1-68570-003-4 (paperback)
ISBN 978-1-68570-004-1 (digital)

Christian Faith Publishing
832 Park Avenue
Meadville, PA 16335
www.christianfaithpublishing.com

Printed in the United States of America

To the three people who helped to create my story but sadly could not live long enough to see it retold in a book—my mother, Elizabeth, my wife, Evelyn, and my sister, Beatrice. May heaven help them to remember the story they know so well!

C O N T E N T S

PREFACE

As an immigrant, educator, scientist, church leader, and a missionary, some of my students, parents, colleagues, friends, and fellow believers have asked me the reason behind my faith, tenacity, and career multiple times. Their questions include, "Where are you originally from?" "How did you get here?' "Why did you become a professor and water chemist?" "When and how did your faith journey begin?" For career reasons, I have visited eighteen different countries and sojourned in five of them outside my own. Everywhere, the questions have been the same. A few years ago, while leading a mission trip of college students to my native Ghana, one of the chaperones asked something probably deeper than I had previously encountered. *"Why do you want to take students more than four thousand miles away to serve and preach Jesus?"* *"What is most important to your life?"* she inquired.

After that day, I began to think more deeply about how I might document my experiences to inspire a response about what is most important in life. The result is this book titled *Transcended*. Some writers may employ more modern media sources (e.g., digital) to address their audiences. Nevertheless, I have chosen a hard copy because of its appeal to traditional audiences. Some writers tell stories about important moments in their lives, some try to seek self-understanding, and others merely try to entertain their readers. *Transcended* goes beyond all these. The book is crafted to inspire readers that although human life is replete with niggly and annoying challenges, success is possible beyond expectation if one has impeccable belief in perseverance and God's restoration power.

Aside from several enthralling personal stories, *Transcended* is couched in a narrative that reveals the complex intersection between faith, social construct, and academic career transformed to touch people's lives with or without material wealth or personal endowments. The book does not only accentuate dedication to Christian higher education, youth mentorship, and "reverse missions" but also touches on simple coaching methods I have and continue to use to help vulnerable immigrants to improve their lives and their families. Most educators agree that we learn best when we relate new information to what we already know. In addition, experts in writing theory believe that expressive, autobiographical writing plays a part in all writing, including academic writing. Still, others argue that the personal voice should be present even in traditional academic discourse, concluding that knowledge and argument must always be personal. The book borrows from these approaches.

Notice that much of the information here is factual. The book relies heavily on the writer's expert knowledge, having told some of the stories orally multiple times before. Nevertheless, some of the historical data and information has been referenced from secondary sources, part of which includes Africa's political and cultural history. These resources are deeply appreciated. Writing the book itself was no mean challenge. It has been postponed several times because of time constraints. Retelling small details of childhood events, for instance, was particularly difficult than originally anticipated. Fortunately, some family members chipped in. Still, that did not happen without frustration. In 2020, millions of people worldwide suffered severe anxiety and heartaches from the ravages of COVID-19; I was no exception. Thankfully, that period of excruciated isolation gave birth to the book, giving credence to the Holy Scriptures that *"the testing of your faith produces perseverance." (James 1:3 NIV)*. In Africa, our elders say, "Misfortunes are a blessing in disguise." This is a running theme in the book. Nothing is unachievable if one remains a persistent swimmer in the flowing grace of God.

1

Soul Day

Her due date was close. Moreover, she missed her mother profoundly. She was desperate to get to her village before late. Night was falling, and finding transport was near impossible. The only passenger wooden truck to the village departed hours before. Her best chance was to travel on her husband's eighteen-wheeler timber-hauling truck. How could a heavily pregnant woman mount such a clumsy old elevated Albion truck? Slowly she trudged into the passenger seat while her sleepy little daughter dozed off on a tiny pillow over the hot inner-engine hood. The young couple was poor. They lived in a small hall-and-chamber room at CPC in Kumasi. Kumasi is the second-largest city in Ghana and the provincial capital of the ancient Ashanti Empire. At the heart of Kumasi is Manhyia town, which hosts the palace, offices, and museum of the famous Ashanti kings. Otumfoɔ Sir Osei Agyeman Prempeh II was the king at the time.

In those days, most pregnant women living in big towns traveled to their villages to deliver their babies. The intention was to receive pre- and postnatal care, emotional support, and new-baby care from their experienced mothers and grandmothers. In Africa, support from the extended family and sometimes the whole village is part of everyday culture. As a trucker, the young man spent most of his time on the road. Therefore, his wife's decision to deliver their baby at the village was great relief. Was that the primary reason behind his ecstasy? Probably not. His wife's absence presented a new opportunity for romance with mistresses' men of his kind publicly described as second, third, or fourth wives. The idea of giving birth in the village was not an easy decision; the young wife was cajoled into such a choice.

Ten days later, a baby boy was born at the village midwife's clinic. That boy was I. Despite looking bouncy, I was still not the healthiest baby. Akan tradition demands that baby boys are circumcised a week or so after birth. In my case, this did not happen. I was deemed too fragile for early circumcision. The native doctor, who incidentally was my maternal uncle, had to apply his potion into my left cheek to help me survive a terrible attack from whooping cough and respiratory distress. An ugly facial scar from this potion has remained one of my nightmarish experiences from childhood until today. I was circumcised only two weeks before baptism at the local AME Zion Methodist Church. Traditionally, christening or baptism happened about ninety days after birth. The only village church was a family church. My grandparents helped to establish it in the 1930s, nearly two decades before Ghana gained independence from the British Empire. As a petty trader, my grandmother and her friends converted into the Methodist Church while on one of their trekking expeditions to coastal towns like Moree (Mowire), Saltpond (Akyemfo), and Elmina (Edina) more than two hundred miles away to purchase sea salt. The new believers and their spouses became some of the earliest missionaries in their local communities.

The Ashanti people of West Africa trace part of their ancestral roots to the Jewish Levitical priesthood. Many of their traditional rites are quite similar with biblical Jewish religious practices, including child-naming ceremonies, circumcision of male babies, preparation of dead bodies for burial, fasting while mourning the dead, menstrual purification, and festival of days and new moons. The Ashantis and their larger Akan relatives have different child-naming and baby-dedication ceremonies depending on their Christian or traditional religious beliefs. The Akans believe, for instance, that babies are gifts from God, just as described in the Jewish and Christian Holy Scriptures.

"Behold, children are a gift of the LORD" (Psalm 127:3 NASB) for "from him and through him and to him are all things" (Romans 11:36). In this first promise, we recognize and honor God as the one who has given us our children. Though it is not always easy, this first promise is a commitment to recognize children as blessings from God and give heartfelt thanks for the privilege of being entrusted by their Creator with the responsibility to raise them in the fear, discipline, and joy of the Lord.

Following traditional norms, "Kwaku" was declared as my first name. Kwaku means "a son born on Wednesday." Therefore, Wednesday is considered my "soul day." Tradition says that God gifted me to my parents on Wednesday. In other words, God created me on Wednesday, which is my "soul day." Prior to colonial rule, Africans hardly recorded days when children were born. Birthdays are a Western legacy. To many West Africans, birthdays are not as important as "soul days." In fact, until the arrival of the slave merchants, colonizers, and Christian missionaries, Africans never required birth certificates for any legal, economic, or financial transactions. The birth of an African child was referenced from significant events such as an earthquake, plague, famine, deluge, or death of a prominent queen mother, chief, or king. Therefore, birthdays or death days passed on to the younger generation through oral tradition. I hardly celebrated my birthday while growing up but no one in my community ever forgot my "soul day" because of my first name. Again, following our African tradition, I was given my full name as "Kwaku Duah" after my father's granduncle who, nearly a century ago, ruled as a subchief (Atipimhene) in the Asantehene's Palace at Manhyia. Atipimhene is one of the war leaders often selected from the lineage of one of the sons of the Asante kings.

Up till now, many churches in Ghana perform infant baptism when babies are about ninety days old. It is not exactly clear why parents have to wait three months before baptizing their babies. There are three possible reasons. The first one relates to church traditions. The diocesan priests visited village churches only three or four times every year to administer the sacrament of baptism. The second is of spiritual significance. The Ashanti people believe that lactating mothers become "spiritually clean" about three months after the birth of a baby (see Leviticus 12). The final reason is medical. After ninety days, they believe that new mothers are substantially free from postpartum complications, making it easy to recommence sexual relations with their spouses. The last two reasons probably applied in my case. Three significant things happened during my christening. First, I was baptized (sprinkled) as a member of the AME Zion Methodist Church family. Second, my date of birth was recorded the first time in the church register. Third, I was given a Christian name.

There are several reasons why many Africans have Christian or English names. In fact, Africans with foreign names are rooted in the history of trade with foreigners, colonization, and religion. Centuries ago, there were no African states like those that we have today. Rather, Africans lived in small tribal communities. Some of them were Ashanti, Oyo, and Benin empires of West Africa. Others were much larger regional states like the Kanem-Bornu Empire of Central Africa, Bantu-Buganda Empire of East Africa, and the Zulu Kingdom in Southern Africa. Europeans (France, Great Britain, Spain, Portugal, and Germany) forcibly grouped the African continent as nations after the great partition of Africa. Since then, European names have become common. Education, Christianity, and Islamic faith are also underpinning factors. Western (Judeo-Christian) and Eastern (Arabica-Islam) names are not a separate thing but intertwined with other cultural legacies including architecture, language, food, and clothing.

Research by historians like Carl Reindorf indicate that European and Arabian missionaries generally viewed African traditional names as heathen for which reason they forced new believers to wear biblical or Arabic-Islamic names. While English-speaking Africans were given English names, French, Portuguese, and Spanish-speaking natives were given names popular among the colonizers. Name changing and name giving was not only a European problem. Many Africans who assumed leadership after the departure of the colonizers also followed the footsteps of their European masters. The Nelson Mandela Foundation has reported, for example, how the original name of Nelson Mandela, the great patriot of Africa, was changed by his African head teacher when he first enrolled in her mission school.

"No one knows why Miss Mdingane chose the name Nelson, although Mandela suggested in his autobiography that he was given the name Nelson after the British sea captain Lord Nelson. Rolihlahla is his birth name given to him by his father."

Something like Mandela's case happened to me. The local pastor called Reverend Kwaku Paul Hanson never recorded birth in his church register or baptized a baby unless a Bible name was chosen. My mother received no formal education and could not read and write. Regardless, she was very smart. Like many of her friends, she memorized and recited several short Bible passages in a highly enthralling way. She was conversant with Bible names and sometimes their meanings. My father's Christian name was Isaiah, but she never wanted that for me. Yes, Isaiah is a good name. But she preferred something completely different. She was always concerned my father had a Christian name without purpose; he was just a Christian in name—no practice. My mother was highly superstitious. She thought taking my father's Christian name might have a negative influence and not make me the type of Christian she wanted me to be. My father was not only an alcoholic but he was also emotionally abusive and highly promiscuous. Like most African women, my mother was cautious about names and their spiritual influence. Reverend Hanson suggested names like Noah, Peter, and Stephen. My mother settled on "Stephen" immediately when she knew the meaning was "fit to wear a crown."

In those days, names and dates of birth recorded in the church register were later used to enroll first graders at the mission school. Reverend Hanson was both the AME Zion Methodist Church minister and head teacher at the school. In line with his pastoral training and church traditions, he created names for nearly every five- to six-year-old enrollee at his school. He simply joined Christian names with their fathers' names as first and last names. What if a child was born with no known biological father? In such cases, he used a male maternal or paternal uncle's name as a surrogate. Last names, surnames, and family names are an enduring Western legacy. In the past,

African children were hardly identified in their communities by their parents' names. Rather, they were identified by their tribal names. Take, for instance, a boy called Kofi Badu. It was easy for people to identify him as a male born on Friday (Kofi), and a tenth-born among his siblings (Badu), or possibly named after a tenth-born male ancestor. Western culture has significantly altered the naming culture of Africans. In my case, my traditional (tribal) name, Kwaku Duah, was not accepted for baptism. So I was registered and baptized as Stephen Opoku. While the minister proposed Stephen, Opoku was referenced to my father. To date, only my family calls me by my tribal name. Later at the Methodist high school, "Duah" was added to my registered name to distinguish me from students with similar names. To Western people, family names are routine culture. To most Africans, family names are a completely borrowed culture.

At age six, I started the local AME Methodist primary school, guided and protected by my older siblings and cousins. While our parents lived and worked in the city of Kumasi, we lived in the village fourteen miles down south, under our grandmother's care.

2

Village Chores

L ike most children, my first day at school was both exciting and
frightening. It was exciting because this was an opportunity to
make friends, play, and learn new things like my older siblings
and cousins. Prior to that, my siblings bragged and teased me regularly with new English words and songs they had learned at school.
That always made me jealous.

"This is my chance to also learn English and songs," I said to
myself confidently at my first day of enrollment.

We stayed in a long queue to be enrolled. Registration was done
by alphabetical last names. My last name, starting with "O," was very
far along the list. I was anxious and impatient. It seemed like my turn
would never come. While Reverend Hanson called out the names, I
clutched tightly to my mother's right arm. Reverend Hanson was my
fear. His loud, imposing voice was intimidating. Before then, I have
heard many weird stories about him from my siblings and cousins.
They gossiped about how stern he was. He was a strict disciplinarian.
They talked about how severely he used his long raffia cane to whip
bullies and students who behaved silly. Sometimes, they demonstrated how students with poor mental skills were lashed and how
impatient he was with children who went to school unkempt and in
untidy uniforms. Beyond that, they resented teachers who punished
students without learning tools like marble counters, crayons, pen-

cils, and workbooks. The thought of my mother leaving me behind to face Reverend Hanson alone nearly choked me.

I sobbed openly when my mother was leaving. I had no choice but to swallow my tears. It was taboo for students to cry at school. Reverend Hanson had no time for pampered kids. He would always yell at crying "fools" into graveyard silence. Was he the wrong man for the job? Probably not. He was strict but a very passionate head teacher. He taught his favorite primary four class, supervised his teaching staff, and managed school matters as if his life depended on it. He gave instructions at the morning assembly, preached sermons at the Wednesday morning chapel, and taught us inspirational Christian hymns. He also taught us how to play indoor and outdoor games like ludo, table tennis, netball, and soccer. He also taught us how to make simple wood and paper crafts, and vegetable and flower gardening. While the male teachers wore a white shirt with matching black shorts and shoes, the female teachers wore cream frocks with matching short-heeled brown shoes. As head teacher, Reverend Hanson always wore his sparkling heavily starched white shirt on top of distinctive baggy pleated white shorts. He matched that with his well-polished, shiny black boots complemented with long woolen socks turned up around his knees. His bushy grayish hair was well-kempt. Moreover, he was clean-shaven every day. He made certain that his students were smartly dressed. He and the other teachers conducted body inspection every Monday morning before classes started almost in a military fashion. They did not only inspect our school uniforms for tidiness but also our hair, teeth, and fingernails. His catchphrase always was "sound mind in a sound body."

In rural Africa, life becomes unbearable for grandparents without their grandchildren to help haul water from the stream, carry firewood for cooking, support farmwork, and run errands. This is part of the reason why we spent our childhood with Grandmother in the village. We assumed she was one of the oldest women in the village. Perhaps we were right. Her physique and facial looks portrayed a mean old woman. Although she was probably in her midfifties, she looked eighty years old because of poverty and poor health. Grandmother was a little woman, barely rising above five feet. She was a lonely widow. She gave birth to a dozen children from her first and second marriages. But I only knew four of my grandmother's children, my mother included. My oldest uncle, the native doctor, died when I was about ten or eleven years old.

Except for Sundays, our grandmother worked tirelessly on her farm. She slashed and burned the bushes, fell trees, uprooted stumps, tilled the soil, and cultivated most of the staple crops we needed. Some of the crops she cultivated included plantains, cassava, cocoyam, yam, beans, and different tropical vegetables. We did not know how and when her farming work started, but we realized how skillful she was with basic principles of shifting cultivation. Part of her unfarmed lots produced a variety of wild fruits including mangoes, papayas, sweet oranges, bananas, pineapples, avocados, and miracle berry. We enjoyed these wild fruits. My favorite fruits were fresh mangoes and papayas. We truly enjoyed the delicious African dishes she prepared daily for dinner.

Our makeshift house was so small for a family with seven children. We battled leaking roofs whenever it rained. On countless occasions, dripping water wetted our mats and pillows while sleeping. Food was scarce, and especially so in the dry season between December and March. There was no running water, electricity, or toilet. We used public latrines, which were filthy, smelly, and unhygienic. The local school was no better. My siblings, cousins, and I walked more than a mile to go to school. We had distinct morning and afternoon school sessions with an hour-and-a-half break when the tropical scorching sun beat our kinky black hair so hard to and from home.

The school sessions were designed to mitigate the intense noontime heat. The brick-walled classrooms were small, roofed with aluminum sheets, fully packed, and hugely suffocating with little fresh air through tiny window shutters. The school had no toilets, fence wall, or security. At night, the school block was at the mercy of thieves, drug abusers, and stray animals. Before classes started every morning, we spent the first hour cleaning our classrooms, the school compound, and the teachers' room. The classrooms were dilapidated and overcrowded. The furniture was often broken, and students whose parents could not afford new writing desks or chairs were frequently turned away from school. The students shared old textbooks, many of which either were torn or had missing pages. Our school had no library. We copied notes dictated by teachers and scripted content written on blackboards. Our teachers demanded that we brought basic classroom equipment like chalk, crayons, dusters, and counting sticks because public supplies were frequently unavailable or inadequate.

Lack of basic learning tools frustrated our teachers greatly. The good part was that most of them were highly professional. They were passionate and dedicated to their teaching craft. My fifth-grade teacher was my most favorite instructor. As one of the patrons, he signed me into the Zion Youth Organization (ZYO) (like the American Boy Scouts) which was excellent in teaching lessons of voluntary service, self-discipline, motivation, hard work, sports, and leadership. Boys who joined the ZYO had the extra advantage of joining the reading club. This was a great benefit to me. I made good friends, learned life lessons and sacrificial service, improved my reading and writing, and got the chance to play soccer. My teacher's devotion toward poor boys like me brought enormous possibilities to learn life lessons, stay out of trouble, and be successful. He helped many other students like me. His love for diversity, inclusion, and mentorship was unparalleled.

Homework was a tedious job, not because the assignments were too difficult but because there was no electricity at home to study. We used a kerosene-burning lantern to study at night. Still, this was not always possible. Why? Because one person or another would sometimes need the lantern for something else. Sometimes the lantern was needed to visit the public latrine half a mile away from home. Without a lantern, there was always the danger of being bitten by a poisonous spider, scorpion, or snake while attending to nature's call. So my grandmother insisted on removing the lantern for needs like that. One trouble with homework was that students who came to class the following morning with incomplete homework were punished. The kind teachers punished lazy students by making them clear weedy school gardens using rusty, blunt machetes. The sterner teachers caned stubborn students and truants in their palms or buttocks.

The elementary school was great! We had plenty of time to learn and play. Life in the village itself was extremely hard. In the tropics, night falls before six o'clock in the evening. At night, we played along the narrow village street. Some of the boys bragged and played with their homemade car toys. Some of them also played ball and marble games as well as "Ahurukutu." The girls played games like "Ampe," "Asɔ," and "Tomanto." Ampe is still very popular among young girls in Ghana. Several girls can play the game at the same time, standing in a semicircular ring. Generally, the "game queen" or initiator acts as the "champion" while the rest become "challengers." Only one of the challengers gets to start the game with the champion while the others wait for their turn. Both the champion and the challenger try to jump as high as they could while they clap and skillfully throw one foot forward at a time. The task of the challenger is to correctly predict which foot is thrown by responding with their foot in midair. "Ampe" was always fascinating to the boys, but we just could not play because it was perceived as a girls' game. In Africa, the distinction between gender roles and activities is still part of everyday culture.

The boys built their own car toys using a variety of materials. They used empty cans, wood, raw rubber, and raffia palm fronds. Aside from ball games, "Ahurukutu" was my most favorite game. "Ahurukutu" is a fun challenge game using a piece of cloth. First, the boys tied two ends of a piece of cloth around their waist. Then they tied the remaining ends around their neck while they took off. While in flight, the hot tropical air blew into the cloth, creating a balloon-like "aircraft" behind their backs. The boys then challenged which design made the biggest air balloon and who ran the fastest.

Nighttime storytelling was always exciting. Storytelling was interesting for three reasons. First, there were no gender and age barriers. Second, it was time to hear fascinating "Ananse" stories, and third, learn words of wisdom from elderly village folks. In Ashanti folklore, the "spider," called "Ananse" in the native language, is perceived as the most cunning and greedy person on earth. "Ananse" is believed to be a Wednesday-born. Because of that, his full name is "Kwaku Ananse." That is "Spider, the Wednesday-born." My most favorite time for storytelling was the cool Harmattan nights in December where we made a campfire to keep warm. My mother was a uniquely gifted storyteller. She liked to organize story times during the Christmas holidays. Everyone was welcome to tell his or her stories. The stories always had three unique phases—call to the story, humorous in-between lyrics, and conclusive request for the next story. The following is one of my mother's most favorite stories:

Just as she always did, she shouted loudly with her trademark commanding voice: "The story of the spider so declared!"

The crowd responded with enthusiasm: "Just so declared by you!"

She started.

"Once upon a time, a great famine occurred on all the earth. The famine was so severe that many people died of hunger and thirst. As a result, Kwaku Ananse and his wife, Ɔkɔnɔre Yaa (Beautiful Thursday-born woman), their daughter, Asɔ (Hoe), and their four sons, Ntikuma (Ax-shaped head), Tikedenkeden (Macrocephalous-head), Afurudotwedotwe (Protruded belly), and Nyaankrɔhwiaa (Long tiny-legs), decided to relocate to a far country in search of food and water. After many days of travel, they came across a village where there was a flowing stream. For years, they had not seen any flowing river. 'Surely, there must be plenty of food around here,' said Ananse.

"Ananse and his family decided to settle near the stream. A few days later, Ntikuma cleaned his gun and set out before dawn to hunt for game. He roamed and roamed the forest until he came across a large farm with large barns packed with corn and yams. He looked left and looked right but saw no one.

"He lifted his hands into the heavens and prayed: 'O god of our ancestors, thank you for this good fortune. My family will no longer go hungry. Be blessed, Kwaku Ananse, be blessed, Ɔkɔnɔre Yaa. You will no longer go hungry.' I will gather as much food and run home with the speed of an antelope,' he said.

"He gathered so much food that his sack was about to break. Just before he could haul away his booty, a fierce-looking old man with a scruffy long gray beard, in tattered clothes, suddenly appeared.

'Who are you? And where do you come from?' the man asked. 'Why are you stealing my food? You will die today from my magic potion,' he said.

"'Ntikuma is my name, my lord. The wise man Kwaku Ananse is my father, and we have traveled from a very far country because of the great famine,' he said. 'Please spare my life and let me live and I will be your slave,' Ntikuma pleaded.

"'You will not live unless you can tell the name of my white long beard,' said the old man. 'The day you successfully name my beard, you will haul all the food you want, even if you need food every day,' he added.

"Ntikuma tried unsuccessfully to name the old man's beard. The man then counted up to ten. At the final count without success, he kept Ntikuma prisoner in a large dark dungeon. Day after day, he brought him out so he could name his beard, but without success.

"One night, a beautiful tiny fairy revealed the name of the man's beard to Ntikuma in a dream. The old man was very shocked when Ntikuma named his beard the following morning.

"'My lord, the name of your beard is Atikodie.'

"The door of liberty was finally opened. Ntikuma hurried home with plenty of food. Kwaku Ananse, greedy as he always is, became indignant when he received a ration.

"'Hmmm, Ntikuma,' he said. 'My ancestors gave you so much food, and look, how mean my portion?' he queried.

"Ntikuma tried to persuade his father that more food was on its way, but without success. Ananse decided to go to the old man's farm to haul food himself without Ntikuma's help. He removed so much food that he nearly emptied one of the barns on the farm. Like before, the old man unexpectedly appeared.

"'Who are you, and where are you from?' the man asked.

"'My name is Kwaku Ananse, the wisest man on earth,' he bragged. 'I have come from a far country because of famine to look for food and water,' he added.

"'You will die from my magic potion unless you can name my long white beard,' the old man said.

"Instead of naming the man's beard, Ananse started a song:

"'Atikodie ee! Ntikuma has overcome your magic charm. Wicked old scruffy Atikodie, the tiny fairy has revealed your name. Old foolish Atikodie, my son Ntikuma has finally overcome your magic charm.'

"Fuming with rage, the old man pounced on Ananse and released his magic potion. Immediately, a large herd of fierce-looking dwarfs appeared. They beat Kwaku Anansie to pulp, severed his head, placed the same behind his bottom, and knocked him against the walls of the food barn. His only rescuer was a large cobweb in the corner of the barn."

The story explains why "Ananse the Spider" has no head and always lives in cobwebs. The big lesson is that "greediness breeds disgrace."

School activities, household chores, and nighttime games intensely wore down our skinny frames before bedtime. Still, our grandmother made certain to wake us up at dawn when the cock crowed. We had no toothbrushes or toothpaste. We brushed our teeth with homemade brushes created from plantain fiber stocks beaten with charcoal. Aside from that, we applied small pieces of stick brushes cut from special tropical hardwoods. Incredibly, those homemade dental cleaners were so good that we never developed dental problems and always sported strong healthy teeth. As a chemist, I now understand the teeth-cleansing power of carbon and calcium. My grandmother was no dentist, but somehow, she knew the bad effects of sugar on the teeth and ensured that candies were forbidden at home. Unfortunately, we often sneaked to buy candies on our way to school. Before school, we walked multiple times to haul water from the stream nearly two miles away. We carried water using different sizes of cured gourds, aluminum buckets, or metal containers. We took a cold bath, ate a little breakfast of corn porridge (sometimes without sugar), and run to school. The teachers were very strict. Students who arrived late were punished.

There were no school meals. We went home during midafternoon break to eat lunch. The morning session lasted from 8:00 a.m. until noon while the afternoon session started at 1:00 p.m. and finished at 3:30 p.m. The break was quite short, yet we completed many different chores. Quite often, we ate a quick lunch of cooked plantain or cocoyam with "kontomire" vegetable sauce, hauled water for our teachers, and rushed back to class. But sometimes we trekked to our grandmother's farm nearly two miles away, ate lunch with her, hauled firewood home, cleaned our sweat, and rushed back to school.

As noted above, my primary school experience was good but still stressful. I loved to go to school and loved to learn new things. I enjoyed playing with my friends and loved many of the teachers. Some of my favorite routines were the Wednesday morning chapel, physical education in the morning, and games on Friday afternoon. Reverend Hanson was a very good storyteller. He told many different Bible stories about Abraham, Moses, David, Jesus, and the twelve apostles. The ones I loved most were the spiritual battles by men of courage, including Joshua, David, and Samson. I was particularly fascinated by the strength in Samson's bushy hair and his conquest over the Philistines. We got the chance to learn traditional and Christian songs. What was even more exciting was the chance to win book prizes for Bible recitals.

The boys often played soccer while the girls played netball. Girls' netball is very popular in English-speaking West Africa. Netball is like basketball, but player roles and rules are significantly different. Just like in Britain, netball is still a girls' game in Ghana. Until recently, girls hardly played soccer in my country. Something bizarre happened one Friday afternoon during the games period. I was about nine years old. Our class teacher decided to experiment a soccer game with mixed teams. This was a crazy idea because the majority of the girls had never kicked a soccer ball. Besides, they knew nothing about the rules of the game. Regardless, we obliged and had fun with that. Before long, many of the girls were exhausted and decided to quit except a couple of them. While dribbling my way toward the opposing goal post, one of the girls unexpectedly charged and knocked me down unconscious, opening a deep cut in my right eyebrow. That is all I could remember. When I regained consciousness, I saw my head heavily bandaged and soaked with blood. I lay on a small wobbly wooden bed at the village clinic in agonizing pain.

My mother and grandmother sat close by on a little black bench with anguished-looking faces. The clinic had no doctor, nurse, or pharmacy. It was manned by one old medical assistant called Uncle Ben and assisted by a "nurse" he trained himself. Uncle Ben had no real experience in treating head injuries or concussions. This worried my mother greatly. Her greatest fear was that I could lose my eye if no skilled care was received. I overheard her in intense discussion with Uncle Ben. But I did not fully understand what was going on. After a while, the man wrote a referral note so that my mother could take me to the district hospital. But how could she afford the cost of treatment? She had enough money to travel ten miles to the district hospital but not enough to pay for the cost of treatment. My grandmother suggested another option.

"Why don't we take him to see his uncle, the native witch doctor?" she asked.

"Such a bad cut close to his eyes can only be treated by a doctor, not the witch doctor," said my mother.

"I have seen your brother solve worse problems," Grandmother insisted.

After arguing for a while, I was taken to see the witch doctor.

"He is badly injured," he said. "But he will be all right," he assured firmly.

Over several weeks, I underwent a slowly painful healing process from herbal treatments. Fortunately, I was nursed back to normal health, saving my badly bruised eye. How I survived that injury was a near miracle.

The primary school was fun. But I dreaded cane lashing and bullies. The school was full of bullies. I was little and skinny. Because of that, I regularly suffered bullying at the hands of some of the bigger boys. I remember one boy who hated me badly and tried to provoke me all the time without reason. He was much bigger than most of the boys in my class. I was very scared of him. One of my cousins, Willie, who often protected me and I thought could face the bully was probably even more scared of him. Coming home after school one afternoon, the big bully kicked my calf, unprovoked, while his friends cheered him on. They called me names, knowing I was so afraid to fight back. When Willie tried to intervene, the boy kicked him harder than he did to me. I was miserable. I felt like crying. Suddenly, I mustered courage, put down my books, and started kicking him back. I managed to beat him so hard that from that day, I earned the nickname Checker.

3

The Parade Dream

Inspiration from my teachers when growing up was huge. But like biblical Timothy, my mother and grandmother's influence was without compare. My mother made certain to instill self-discipline, hard work, respect for family values, and faith in God. Though uneducated, her philosophy about good education was spotless. On countless occasions, she would yell at me to complete my homework while boys of my age played games on street corners after school.

There is one story I will never forget. I was very passionate about soccer. But I was not alone; many African boys are passionate about soccer for good reasons. The game of soccer is arguably the most fun for African boys. Besides, the community that soccer brings is arguably the greatest among all games. Additionally, sports are one of the best ways for young people to stay healthy and out of trouble. No wonder some of the most gifted African players have developed professional careers in soccer, earning enormous incomes in Europe and across the globe. African boys play soccer with nearly everything they can find. In addition, they tend to play soccer on nearly every street or corner. In their neighborhoods, they play soccer with green hard oranges, avocado seeds, tins covered with latex, rolled rags, plastics, and rubber balls. Soccer is the biggest sport in most schools in Africa. There are hardly any properly constructed soccer or training fields. Still, many of the boys try to create their own makeshift playgrounds. When I was growing up, the boys who owned rubber or leather soccer balls were considered rich. One needed to be in their good books before they could play.

When I was in middle school, soccer matches were generally played on Sunday mornings and afternoons. I played matches on Sunday afternoon because morning church services were mandatory for my family. My mother would never allow me or any of my cousins to skip church for soccer games. One Sunday morning, however, our youth coach persuaded me to play a match he thought we could lose if I did not play. He was insistent not because I was exceptionally good but because many of the playing squad were unavailable because of church. I skipped church to play. We won and proceeded to the championship final. I could not escape punishment for failing to show up at church. My mother withheld food from me until evening time. Going hungry all day because I ducked church service was a huge lesson. Since then, I never skipped church, not even when I was sick. God's sanctuary was everything to my mother. Even when sick, she made us believe that the church was the best place for sick people to receive healing. Later in life, I recognized the sanity in her spiritual beliefs. My story is proof that physical, spiritual, emotional, financial, and psychological healing only comes from God. As a boy, my mother insisted on church, education, and self-discipline. Today, these values have shaped my personality and academic career.

How did my academic career begin? I first arrived at the Methodist Boys' boarding high school when I was about fifteen years old. One of the greatest needs after Ghana's independence in 1957 was the development of human capital to create an economic muscle. High school education expanded substantially when I was growing up. The political leaders after independence, led by Osagyefo Dr. Kwame Nkrumah (Ghana's first president), were determined and serious about educational opportunities. The starting point was the free compulsory primary and middle school education and the establishment of the Ghana Educational Trust. Several authors like Moses K. Antwi (1992), Albert Adu Boahen (2000), Kwame Akyeampong (2010), and Samuel Adu-Gyamfi, et al. (2016) have documented the history of Ghana's educational reforms after the country's independence. Dr. Nkrumah's greatest legacy was the establishment of the Ghana Educational Trust in 1958. In September 1961, his government started the free and compulsory primary and middle school education for all children of school-going age. By 1959, the number of primary schools increased from 3,571 to 3,713. At the same time, 83 middle schools were added to the existing 1,311. When Ghana became a republic in 1960, 59 new public high schools were built as part of the Ghana Educational Trust, resulting in a tremendous increase in student enrollment. According to Adu Boahen, the expansion of teacher training resulted in the establishment of the National Teacher Training Council in 1958, which was tasked with superintending the training, remuneration, and professional development of teachers. At the same time, two new university colleges were established, being the University College of the Gold Coast (1948), and the Kumasi College of Arts, Science, and Technology (1952). The University College of Cape Coast was later built in 1962. The first two universities have now been renamed as University of Ghana and Kwame Nkrumah University of Science and Technology, respectively.

Tuition fees for public schools have been free since Ghana's independence. Still, children from poor families could never pursue high school education unless their parents could afford the cost of boarding and lodging fees. Until the last couple of years, it was cheaper to pay for university education than high school in Ghana. Why that was the case is still difficult to understand. However, the colonial creation of a class system was partly to blame. The political elites and rich executives made it extremely hard for children from poor families to compete with their wards by entrenching the expensive boarding school system. My parents were too poor to pay for my high school education. The thought of that distressed me anytime the West African Common Entrance Examination approached. Up until now, middle school students across West Africa must pass a subregional examination to enter high school. I was scared about that examination not because of lack of ability but because poverty was likely going to block my access. I discussed these many times with one of my teachers. Mr. Daniel was a great mentor to many students. One day, while engaged in a conversation with him, he said to me:

"You don't have to worry too much. Just work hard and score some of the highest marks on the common entrance examination," he said. "If you did better than most of your peers, you will qualify for Government of Ghana scholarship which will take care of everything you need, and your parents won't have to pay," he concluded.

This is exactly what happened. My teacher knew I would probably not afford the registration fees, so he paid for that and helped me to complete the registration forms. About three months later, I joined a bunch of students to write the examinations in the nearest West African Examinations Council (WAEC) Center. The test was composed of middle school level mathematics, English language, and verbal and quantitative aptitude test. We did not receive the results until about three months later. One morning, some students and I were summoned to the head teacher's office. I was scared. Students who were called to the head teacher's office were often greeted with bad news. Sometimes, they were punished for violating school rules. Other times, they were summoned to the office because the head teacher had received some bad report about them from home. That day was different. There was good news. My examination scores were one of the best in the entire district. Mr. Daniel was surprised I was not as excited as the other students who passed the test. There was a reason why I was downcast. There was no Government of Ghana scholarship letter attached to my results. Without that, there was no way I could go to high school. Not long afterward, the long summer vacation began. That was the time many students prepared for high school enrollment. Some of my friends talked excitedly about their preparations. After listening to them, I went home and cried quietly. Gradually, my mother started noticing changes in my mood. I could no longer hide my frustration.

One day, I asked her, "Why are we were so poor that I can't go to high school even though I achieved one of the best scores at the common entrance examination?"

"The Lord will provide," she said sadly. After that, she intelligently removed eye contact with me.

When my father returned from one of his long road trips, Mother pleaded hard for him to pay my admission deposit worth nearly eight US dollars. The high schools charged admission deposits for two reasons. First, to reserve slots for incoming freshmen, and second, to provide students with an enrollment prospectus. The students' prospectus was a paper document that listed all educational and personal requirements for enrollment into the boarding school. I checked a copy of one of my friends' prospectus, and it listed things like boarding and lodging fees, textbook and stationery fees, prescribed school uniforms, dormitory clothes, student mattresses, bedding sets, metal trunks, and wooden ("chop") boxes. In addition, the list included a bucket, machete, toiletries, and a host of other personal items.

"How could my parents afford all these things?" I asked myself. For days, I was depressed and hardly talked to anyone, but I never stopped praying to God.

I felt a huge sigh of relief when my father finally agreed to pay my admission deposit. Along with my cousin, Akowuah, we went to the school to pay my enrollment deposit. Akowuah was about four years older than I was and was a senior in another coeducational boarding school. Because of excitement, I kept asking him several unimportant questions about high school until he was probably too bored to answer me.

"Now this is my chance," I said to myself confidently.

Yes, we were poor but I also knew that if my father were to quit drinking, refrained from promiscuity, and remained family-focused, he could afford to see me through high school. Was that going to happen? I had my doubts. He seemed to care more about himself than us. The best part was that my admission was reserved. Besides, I had a students' prospectus just like my other friends. The bad part was that my admission documents still showed no Government of Ghana scholarship. My life depended on public financial support. Many weeks passed, and my father never arrived home from his road trip. My mother woke up every day at dawn to pray. She believed in miracles. Still, I felt her sense of despondency. I knew my situation was affecting her. Anytime I heard her pray, tears filled my eyes.

In September, when the new academic year commenced, I could not enroll as I had hoped to. One night, I had a strange dream. In the dream, I saw a large group of students, security personnel, and many people marching briskly at the sports stadium. I do not fully remember everything. But I remember the event was like an Independence Day parade. In Ghana, Independence Day celebrations (March 6) are often observed along with elegant parades by students, workers, and security personnel. I was in a large crowd in the stands, cheering loudly. I saw the students smartly dressed in their uniforms and marching gracefully in response to military music. Unexpectedly, I saw my primary school head teacher, Reverend Hanson, in his usual sparkling white uniform. He walked up to me and said:

"Here, take it. Hoist the flag. You are one of the school prefects."

I protested and said, "No, I am not one of the students. I have no uniform."

Reverend Hanson insisted. I took the large Ghana flag and started descending the staircase. Suddenly, my eyes opened, and I heard my mother praying.

About a week later, I received a letter in the mail from my high school headmaster saying that his school has reopened three weeks earlier so if I failed to show up the following week, my Government of Ghana scholarship award would be transferred to another student on his waiting list. I nearly fainted!

"How?" I questioned myself. "Nobody ever told me about a scholarship award." I stood perplexed. Unknown to me, I had been awarded the Ghana Cocoa Board high school scholarship because of my common entrance examination scores. I never knew I had to report to the school before it could take effect. I assumed some letter or document would be sent to confirm this. My family was completely ignorant. I was sitting home brooding in great pain.

I ran like a bull to inform my mother. She was busy washing and drying clothes behind our house. She burst into indescribable joy. She sang, danced, and worshipped God. It was as if she had won a jackpot. She dispatched me to inform my older sister called Beatrice. We still call her "Auntie B" in our family. My mother asked whether she could purchase the items listed in my prospectus. This was the problem. The total cost of the prospectus was probably greater than Auntie B's wages for six months. Her wages as a store girl were incapable of buying a quarter of the things I needed. Auntie B was and still is a very generous woman. She and Mother came up with a plan. They sold several of their personal belongings to help me beat the headmaster's deadline.

The Methodist Boys' boarding school was regimental. Its academic and social organization were expertly regulated. The students were highly competitive. The behavioral ethics, dress code, and schedules were observed with near-military precision. The boys studied very hard day and night. Although the high school curriculum was countrywide, our headmaster and his staff hugely emphasized general science, mathematics, English language, music, and visual art. Leadership, spiritual formation, and sports were also accentuated.

Boarding schools in Ghana have strict routines. In Africa, bells and drums are a symbol of community attention. Our high school was not different. Different sounds of the drum represented call for different things. There was a rising bell and one for bedtime. There was a bell for chapel, classes, dining, siesta, games, and nighttime homework that we called prep time. Africans are notoriously poor timekeepers. What many Western people deride as the "African time" is a legendary problem. This was never the case in my boarding school. Students who were habitual latecomers were continuously in trouble. They were punished severely. African traditions were a big part of our education. It was against school rules to appear unkempt. For instance, students were not allowed to appear in the classroom or at a school function in untidy clothes, baggy trousers, unlaced shoes, or unbuckled sandals. While we wore light-blue shirts over khaki shorts for classes, we were not admitted into the dining hall (cafeteria) unless we wore white shirts over khaki trousers. For Sunday church service, it was mandatory for the students to wear a school tie with matching black shoes or a traditional African cloth. Church services were compulsory, and absenting oneself put them in serious trouble.

I come from a family of music lovers. I learned to sing in the local church choir at about age eleven. That experience got me recruited into the high school's "Male Voices' Choir." Freshmen like me were trained to sing soprano and alto. This was an opportunity to learn the piano. Before long, I was one of the school pianists along with my best friend, Alex. Church services with officiating pastors like Reverend Boadi from the Kumasi Baptist Seminary was spiritually stimulating. But one of the most unforgettable weekend routines was dormitory inspection. Four things characterized the monthly Saturday morning inspection. A team comprising the senior housemaster, tutor-on-duty, senior school prefect, and sanitary prefect conducted it. It was mandatory for all students to first tidy their dormitories, make their beds with clean white sheets, and maintain a clean compound. Every corner was expected to be spotlessly clean. We were required to scrub the bathrooms and toilets. After which we were expected to have a shower, dress up in our white uniforms, and be ready for inspection. This was no mean competition between the dormitories. Points were awarded for excellent performance, and points deducted for insufficient cleanliness. Woe unto any dormitory that came last in the inspection. They were punished to clear overgrown bushes hugely populated with tall elephant grasses. This was probably one of the harshest punishments on campus. The students euphemistically called the area Siberia because of its outstretched fallow land.

I was appointed the prefect responsible for the dining hall (cafeteria) in my senior year. Boarding school cafeterias in Ghana are akin to high schools in the US. The kitchen and pantry, headed by a professional matron, is part of the general school operations system. In our school, the senior housemaster, who is the third in command in the administrative chain, oversaw the cafeteria operations. A senior student was appointed to manage the dining hall and to liaise between the administration, the kitchen staff, and the student body. Initially, the headmaster preferred one of the "bigger" boys because from his experience, managing the dining hall was probably the hardest job among the prefects. After a brief interview in his office, however, he was convinced about my ability to cope with the demands of the job. The headmaster was right. The senior school prefect and dining hall perfect jobs were the most demanding of all the student government positions. There were more than six hundred boys. They appeared never satisfied with any of the prepared meals. They constantly complained about poor meals. One of my jobs was to ensure that the meals were nutritious and adequate in quantity. While the kitchen staff prepared meals for breakfast, lunch, and dinner, contracted companies delivered many food supplies. The Bantama Electric Bakery, one of the largest bakeries at that time in the city of Kumasi, supplied our bread. Unfortunately, those were the days Ghana had started experiencing famine and economic downturn under military dictatorships.

One fateful morning, our bread for breakfast was found contaminated with gasoline. Because of the mistrust between the students and the school administration, they perceived that was a deliberate poisoning attempt by the kitchen staff. I tried to explain the possible circumstances and expressed my plan to address the problem. What happened afterward was regrettable. A notorious student riot erupted. There was so much damage to school property that the school was closed. When the city police tried to intervene, a nasty confrontation ensued. All the student leaders were detained in jail for nearly twenty-four hours. The security agencies blamed the student government for the riots, but thankfully, the school administration vouched for our innocence. When my mother heard about my incarceration, she nearly passed out. Eventually, we were released, but the school remained closed for weeks. We all signed a bond of good behavior and paid for the cost of damages before academic work resumed. This was a horrifying experience. I learned good lessons about leadership, interpersonal communication, and circumspection amid crises.

Science is part of my nature now. I express scientific ideas in various engagements—my classroom, at home, and even at church. I remember while teaching ninth-grade general science at the Tudor Grange High School in North East England years ago, one of my students got upset because I did not allow him to complete his social studies project during my chemistry class. When I asked him to put his work away, he screamed, saying: "As for you, all you care about is science, science, science." The entire classroom was thrown into a fit of laughter. This is still a big joke among teachers at Tudor Grange School.

I do not exactly remember when and what motivated my passion for science. But I still recall my fascination with scientific discoveries when I was a little boy. I liked to read books and articles about James Watt and his invention of the steam engine, Sir Isaac Newton and his apple-gravity experiments, air navigation by the Wright brothers, and space explorations by Russian and American astronauts. These stories were great, but nobody better engendered my interest in science than an American Peace Corps teacher called Ms. Zamwari. The lady greatly inspired me while a sophomore in high school.

Ms. Zamwari was a passionate, dedicated, and highly captivating teacher. I remember she was an English and history teacher. But I also recall her rich knowledge of science. During the last term of the academic year, our general science tutor got seriously ill and stayed away for several weeks. One morning, Ms. Zamwari was introduced as our substitute tutor for science.

"What?" some of the boys exclaimed. "We thought Ms. Zamwari was an English tutor. How could she substitute for general science?" they queried. After a couple of lessons, we all agreed that she explained science much better than our regular teacher did. She did not only teach us science but she also detailed the history behind scientific theories, related science to everyday life, and carried out fascinating demonstrations, explaining how science and technology had shaped the developed world. My love for science amplified thereafter.

Ms. Zamwari was a very pretty woman. She was possibly of Middle Eastern or Hispanic descent. She looked quite young, probably only a few years older than students did in the senior class. Our school had only three female teachers. So like the others, Ms. Zamwari was highly regarded. She was not only a good teacher but she was also very generous. She provided snacks, soccer balls, and school supplies to some of the students she considered poor. Something incomprehensible happened one day. One of the senior students who was assigned to her as an errand boy sneaked into her bedroom while she was sleeping and half-naked. Overcome by lust, he attempted to rape the teacher. Ms. Zamwari successfully freed herself and reported the crime to the school authorities. Our headmaster was incredibly stern.

The students nicknamed him "Agaja." Agaja was one of the wicked kings of the ancient Dahomeyan Empire in West Africa. As students, we deliberately equated his demand for strict discipline with wickedness. The student vehemently denied having caused any trouble. Our headmaster was never the type to be fooled. He sacked the student from the school. The boy's silly action broke the hearts of many of the students. The attack so haunted Ms. Zamwari that she left our school. That was the last time we heard about her.

Ultimately, I passed the double regional high school examinations (General Certificate of Education—Ordinary and Advanced Levels) to enter the then University of Science and Technology in Kumasi to pursue engineering science. After graduation, I passed a competitive examination that won me a fellowship award to pursue graduate studies, first in the Netherlands, then later in the United Kingdom. The details of these achievements are the subject of subsequent chapters.

4

Downtown Slums

If a young person survived the inner-city slums of Asawasi, they probably would survive in any other part of the world. Asawasi is the epitome of hard city life. The district is characterized by crime, gambling, drugs, child prostitution, alcohol, disease, poverty, and physical abuse.

During Christmas or Ramadan, we had plenty of delicious food to eat. That was about all. For the most part, we struggled for everyday necessities. I do not exactly know how my grandmother (my father's mother) acquired our tiny brick "passenger" house. That is where our family of fifteen people lived. The address at E-Line housed my grandmother, my father's younger sister, and her seven children plus grandchildren, my father, stepmother, and myself. Our house is less than three miles southeast of the famous Manhyia Palace. Some of the most populous Muslim communities in Ghana—Akwatia Line, Alabar, Sabon Zongo, Aboabo, and Sawaaba—surround Asawasi. Hausa (popular West African language) is the most dominant language among Muslim populations in Ghana. Most children raised in Asawasi can speak Hausa in addition to other Ghanaian languages. Sadly, I have now lost proficiency in Hausa over the passage of time.

My grandmother, auntie, and stepmother sold foodstuff at the sprawling Kejetia market. Aside from Nigeria's Ibadan, the Kejetia market is arguably the largest open market in West Africa. One experiences daily frenetic scenes in open African markets. Kejetia is no exception. Saturday was, and is still, a big market day. Before sunrise, one could see convoys of clumsy mummy trucks off-loading a variety of goods—foodstuff, fish, live animals, cooking oil, clothing, shoes, and local farm implement. Traditionally, rural women sold farm produce cultivated by their spouses. Sadly, they made less money compared to their urban counterparts. While they hurried to dispose of their produce and products before the market closed, their city counterparts warehoused goods in stalls to make a better retail profit. One can find nearly everything at the Kejetia market, and a wide range of skillful artisans endeavor to fix all kinds of broken things in tiny shops. There are watch and clock repairers, dressmakers, cobblers, metal and plastic workers, masons, electricians, carpenters, jewelers, and mechanical fitters. The Kejetia leather industry (shoes, bags, purses, and wallets) is legendary. The industry attracts traders across the West African subregion including Nigeria, Togo, Benin, Ivory Coast, Mali, and Benin. My family sold plantains for a living. When my grandmother grew too old with eye problems, some of my female cousins filled her place. My family's market traditions have continued until today. We helped hauling foodstuff from the lorry station whenever we came home for summer vacations. We sometimes carried food and groceries home, walking several miles away.

Overcrowding was one of the biggest problems at Asawasi. Majority of homes had no running water or toilet facilities. Most people used stinky, unhygienic public latrines. The latrines lacked proper care and maintenance. The stench from the sewage sludge badly polluted the environment, leading to waterborne diseases like malaria, typhoid fever, and cholera. There was not a single day we did not suffer mosquito bites and resultant malaria fever. I was one of the most vulnerable in my entire family.

Attending church was not very different from my previous experience in the village. My grandmother was a devout Methodist, but my auntie and her children were all Muslims. My auntie was married to a man from her village who was sarcastically referred to as an Asante Muslim. My father and stepmother never attended church. Not living with my mother at that time was a big challenge. My stepmother was notoriously selfish. Many times, she tried to create problems when my father was away on his long trucking trips. Later, I understood the spiritual significance of her obnoxiousness. That forced me out of the house to spend more time at the church when school was on vacation.

I have already mentioned Ghana's political and economic problems between 1972 and 1992. It is necessary to discuss some details here. There were repetitive military coups, economic mismanagement, drought, and famine. On January 13, 1972, Col. I. K. Acheampong (later Gen. Acheampong) toppled the Dr. K. A. Busia Progress Party government in a coup d'état and instituted the Supreme Military Council (SMC). The only positive thing about Gen. Acheampong's administration was its agricultural program titled Operation Feed Yourself (OFY). The OFY was an aggressive campaign for citizens to embark on farming to boost food production. The campaign was spearheaded by Col. Bernasko, the then-Commissioner for Agriculture. The program was a big success. While the local population positively responded to the OFY, the country was blessed with rains and bumper harvest in the mid-1970s. Unfortunately, the political instability continued with military regimes. One of the most notorious failures of Gen. Acheampong's leadership was his lack of economic acuity and unbridled promiscuity. The dictator was rumored to have gifted large infrastructure contracts, public property, and money to several women who satisfied his sexual needs. Later, he attempted a big political trick on the country with a convoluted idea of "Union Government" aimed at entrenching political power. Despite a lavish political campaign, the Ghanaian population saw through his deceit and massively rejected the idea when a national referendum was conducted in 1977. This followed a series of military coup d'états including SMC II by Gen. Edward Akufo (1978), Armed Forces Revolutionary Council by Flight Lt. Jerry John Rawlings (May 15 and June 4, 1979), and Provisional National Defense Council (PNDC) on December 31, 1981, again by J. J. Rawlings. These military takeovers were briefly interspersed by the elected administration of Dr. Hilla Limann, leader of the Peoples' National Party (PNP). The PNP was an offshoot of the Convention People's Party, originally founded in 1949 by Dr. Kwame Nkrumah. Amid these upheavals, nearly two million Ghanaians who had previously sought economic refuge in Nigeria during the country's oil boom were deported back home—the so-called Agege Returnees problem.

The socioeconomic burden brought on by the Nigerian deportation was incalculable. Food was scarce, and nearly every essential commodity was in short supply. There was no rice, corn, plantain, cassava, vegetables, fruits, meat, or fish. We stayed in very long queues for hours to purchase basic items like soap, toothpaste, bread, milk, and sugar. These items were classified as "essential commodities" and could only be sold in special public stores called People's Shops. The People's Shops were created by the military government because the local traders hoarded essential commodities and retailed later for big profits. If the security agencies apprehended the hoarders, they were severely brutalized. The media was full of stories where women violators (then called economic saboteurs) were stripped naked in public and severely assaulted by marauding soldiers. Still, supplies were gravely limited. Fighting for essential commodities at the People's Shops was a question of survival of the fittest. The older people, women, and young children were the worst affected. Many strong men heckled others to get to the front of the queue. This called for more trouble when the military, police, or the "revolutionary" militia, called the Committee of Defense of the Revolution (CDR), were called to restore order. Multiple times, I saw shoppers severely assaulted by the security personnel. Unfortunately, many of these public officers were themselves corrupt. Frequently, they looted the supplies unashamedly and favored their families and friends in the queues.

Droughts in Africa are cyclical and generally driven by climate variability. Ghana sits above the equator and experiences an alternating wet and dry season each year. The movement of the Intertropical Convergence Zone (ITCZ) influences the climate of West Africa. This zone is an area of low pressure that forms where the northeast trade winds meet the southeast trade winds near the earth's equator. As these winds converge, moist air is forced upward. This causes water vapor to condense. As the air cools and rises, it results in a band of heavy precipitation. The band moves seasonally, always being drawn toward the area of most intense solar heating, or warmest surface temperatures. It moves toward the southern hemisphere from September through February and reverses direction in preparation for northern hemisphere summer that occurs in the middle of the calendar year. As a result, Ghana is characterized by hot, dry, and dusty harmattan winds from high-pressure cells of the Azores that meet cold moist "monsoon" winds from the south Atlantic anticyclones. The timing, intensity, and duration of the ITCZ over the area determine the amount and duration of rainfall. Rainfall is heaviest (~2500 mm) in the forested humid south and decreases northward along a latitudinal gradient in the Sahel savanna region (sometimes as low as 650 mm per year).

The radiative changes were believed to be the cause of the West Africa droughts from about 1976 until about 1984. The droughts and famine resulted in the catastrophic demise of people and livestock. Those who survived suffered serious starvation manifested by bony clavicles which people sarcastically called Rawlings chains. The then-thirty-two-year-old Ft. Lt. J. J. Rawlings was the head of state. Out of superstition, some people believed Rawlings was a bad omen and the cause of the famine. Occasionally, my father brought home some food upon return from his road trips. Unfortunately, my stepmother secretly stored the food for her own relatives while I went hungry for several days. A few of the hard famine stories are worth recounting here.

One of our neighbors returned from Ivory Coast with a large quantity of corn. Her name was Daavi, which means "young woman." Daavi was a kenkey seller. Kenkey is a Ghanaian dish made from cooked semifermented corn dough wrapped in dry corn husks. Kenkey is served with hot pepper sauce garnished with sliced onions and fresh tomatoes and served with fried or smoked tilapia fish. Kenkey in large quantities takes two to three hours to cook. Daavi's kenkey was often ready before 6:00 a.m. Her food was a hotcake. We spent much of the night in her small house while she prepared fresh dough. It was impossible to get kenkey if one did not wait to buy the dough before it was cooked. We stayed in Daavi's hallway all night to get one ball of kenkey, and such was the severity of the famine.

The second story concerns one strange weather condition in 1983. We woke up one morning to find that smoke had engulfed the entire city of Kumasi. There was darkness for nearly three days. We could not breathe; neither could we open our eyes. The smoke was so choking that people were breathless. Shortly afterward, news broke that the smoke had consumed the entire country. We later understood that much of the Guinea and Sahel savanna had been burning for weeks, which had traveled all the way to the coastal regions of West Africa. The news media reported the loss of several lives, but up until today, no one knew exactly how many people perished from that tragedy.

The droughts exacerbated the economic conditions at the time. I hung out with other friends who tried to fix their lives via improper means like pilfering, drugs, alcohol, smoking, and sex. Some of them gleefully shared their experiences with marijuana and shoplifting. Thankfully, a couple of them discussed how to make money through head-porter jobs serving rich Malian and Nigerien maize and cola nut traders. In order not to look silly, I sometimes pretended knowledge about some of the things they talked about while, in fact, I was completely ignorant. I always tried to use my instincts. My mother's advice was always at the back of my mind. She knew a couple of those boys including my half-brother and frequently warned me to stay away from them.

One hot afternoon during the summer vacation, I trekked across town to Auntie B's (my elder sister) house, looking for food. She asked if I would be willing to work as a driver's mate for her husband's mummy truck. The truck was used to haul foodstuff from villages in the Nkawie District, about thirty miles northwest of Kumasi. The local parlance for lorry drivers' mate in Ghana is *aplanke*.

"Sure, that will be good for me," I said. "It will save me from two problems," I said to myself. "First, it will give me money to buy food, and second, save me from hanging out with bad friends," I concluded.

The first three weeks went well. I had money to buy food and purchase a new pair of shoes. The job of an *aplanke* is strenuous and risky. His primary task is the collection and accounting for haulage fees from the passengers. I was responsible for loading and off-load-ing the farm produce. Also, I helped to wash the mud-covered lorry after the day's job. But it is important for an *aplanke* to learn the skill of embarking and disembarking when the truck was in flight. This was a truly hard skill to learn in a couple of weeks. One eve-ning, tragedy struck. I tripped and fell badly on the gravel tarmac while embarking on the truck. I was nearly run over and got heavily bruised. I stayed away for more than two weeks. Upon return, I lost the job with extreme disappointment. Soon, I was back with my friends. We hung out at inner-city disco clubs like Cameo, Freakie-Deakie, Sphinx, and Jatokrom-Annex with some girls. How I man-aged to stay away from drugs, alcohol, and cigarettes is still a mystery. By this time, I had quit praying regularly as I used to. Little by little, I started finding excuses to absent from choir practices. The good part was that I hardly missed Sunday church services. Not long, I began to recognize the wrong direction my life was going. Although my friends were not churched, they admired my interest in church. They perceived I was an uncomfortable fit in their group. I regained a bit of spiritual strength to start regular prayers again.

One day, I was on a municipal bus to visit my mother in her vil-lage when I saw two people (probably in their late twenties) preach-ing about Jesus Christ. Preaching commercial vehicles in Ghana is not illegal. I became interested when they said one of the reasons why Jesus died was to establish his church on earth, citing Matthew 16:18–19. They concluded that the multiplicity of churches was a departure from divine authority. That immediately aroused my curi-osity. I questioned their doctrinal standpoint, which suddenly drew support from some of the passengers. Although I did not agree with the young preachers, I still admired their passion for evangelism. After praying for the passengers, they declared their church affiliation as Church of Christ.

A couple of weeks later while visiting one of my friends, Ben, a couple of miles away from home, I came across a roadside sign-post which read: "Churches of Christ invite You for Bible Studies—Tuesdays at 7:00 p.m." Their meetings were held in a small private school near Osei Kyeretwie High School at Dichemso. I immediately remembered the young preachers on the municipal bus. I decided to check the group out later. That was where I met an elderly man I recognized as a Nigerian because of his looks and English accent. After a lengthy conversation, I realized he was an engine (train) driver and lived only a few blocks away from my house. Brother Stephen was his name. He was about my father's age. He was extremely polite and invited me for a one-on-one Bible study and prayer. I had been raised Methodist, but this was probably the closest I had come regarding serious Bible studies. I jumped at the opportunity. Our friendship grew over time. Even though I went back to the boarding school weeks later, Brother Stephen continued to exchange letters with me while we studied the Bible.

During the summer vacation in 1981, Brother Stephen invited me to the Church of Christ which met in one of the classrooms of the then-Asante Collegiate School near the Baso Club in Asafo-Abrotia. Asante Collegiate was private accountancy and secretarial college owned by one Dr. Roberts, an immigrant from Sierra Leone. I kept postponing Stephen's invitation because I had been made to believe how wrong it was for a Methodist member to visit another church without justifiable reason. One Sunday morning in July 1981, I visited Brother Stephen's church along with Otchere, my cousin and best friend. The preacher's sermon was so inspiring that Otchere and I decided to subject ourselves to baptism. The fellowship was strong, and the spiritual atmosphere was unbelievably compelling. The brethren were genuinely welcoming and truly kind. They sang acapella music with a distinctive echo from the squeezed old classroom they used as a sanctuary. They did not appear rich, yet they worshipped God joyfully. Their Bible class was illuminating and drew many practical applications I immediately found helpful. There were about eighty worshippers including five or six children. The members appeared to know one another closely and seemed to be quite spiritually connected.

Still, I said to myself, "This is the last time I will be here." "I don't want to be part of a weird religious cult like this."

I was wrong. I kept going there because of the strong fellowship and my friendship with Brother Stephen and Brother Frank. They visited me regularly and never stopped studying the Bible with me. At church one Sunday, I saw a young lady who seemed quite familiar. I wanted to talk to her, but I was too shy to do so.

"I am just a new member. And this might seem awkward if I tried to ask her questions," I said to myself.

While catching up with Frank in between Bible class and worship service, I pointed to her and asked if I could talk to her after service. "Of course," said Frank. "Everyone is a family here. We are all brothers and sisters, and we are all children of the same Father, God Almighty, the maker of the heavens and the earth," he added. "I will call her for you, after church if you please. In fact, she is your Asawasi neighbor and lives a few blocks away from your house," Frank said.

That suddenly struck me.

"That is the reason why I know her," I said to myself quietly. After church, Evelyn approached me with a broad smile and asked, "You are a new brother, what is your name, please?"

"My name is Steve," I responded with a smile. A long conversation followed.

When she realized I lived at Asawasi, she asked in a kind voice, "Would you like to join our Dichemso Zone for Bible studies?"

"Most certainly," I responded with strong affirmation. I said to myself quietly, "Which guy will refuse a Bible study request from a charming girl like you?"

Evelyn was extremely beautiful. Her exquisite slim body fully matched her soft shiny skin and fair color complexion. Her smooth rounded lips exceptionally matched her adorable happy smile. She was about seventeen years old when we first met. Before long, I realized she was a commuter high school student near the Kwame Nkrumah University of Science and Technology. There were so many wonderful things about Evelyn. She was smartly dressed, kind, and polite. Her spiritual maturity clearly superseded her physical age. She was a great singer and had an unbelievable knowledge of the scriptures. I had never met a girl like her with such depth of Bible knowledge. Like a pulpit minister, she freely quoted the scriptures from memory. There was not a single biblical question or theological subject she was unfamiliar with. Beyond all this, she possessed a fascinating demeanor with a great sense of humor. Shortly thereafter, I realized she was from a family of church ministers. Two of her uncles were Church of Christ ministers while another was a Methodist priest. Her uncle, Brother Martin, was not only a preacher but also worked in the printing department at the Ghana Bible College. When I probed further, she confirmed she had been a Bible student since age eleven when she first baptized as a Christian. "How remarkable," I said to myself. My friendship with Evelyn grew rapidly. We spent a lot of time hanging out with the church youth group. We trekked for Bible studies and worship services together, and created a Bible outreach group. We created a group to assist with community service projects. We visited each other regularly and became closely acquainted with one another's family.

A couple of years later, our relationship developed from a simple friendship into a romantic one. We began to fall in love with one another deeply. We did not only encourage each other about spirituality and academic excellence but we began to discuss life together, with plans to marry after college. We spent a lot of time studying while we prepared for our high school examinations. While I prepared for my GCE A-Level examinations, seeking to pursue university education, she also prepared for her GCE O-Level, seeking admission into the sixth form school, which is the second tier of high school in Ghana. Just about that time, tragedy struck Evelyn's family. Her mother tragically lost her entire business because of an austere Government of Ghana currency devaluation and redenomination by the military administration. Her mother also lost large sums of money after some military personnel seized her merchandise for hoarding African wax prints. On top of that, their family house was appropriated by court order and auctioned. Because of the fear of incarceration, her mother absconded to Nigeria to join her husband who was there teaching in a high school. Evelyn and her six other siblings suddenly became destitute. She terminated school after her examinations to find work to be able to look after her siblings. I was inconsolable when she confirmed her plans to move to Accra to find work. I was scared that could mark the end of our courtship. Our reconnection a few years later is the subject of subsequent chapters.

5

Disciple of Christ

Brother Stephen is one of the most devoted followers of Christ I have ever known. He took the preaching of the word of God seriously and exhibited an incredible love for missions. His eagerness to lead people to faith was unparalleled. He knew the scriptures very well and quoted Bible passages copiously to make every point he made. He was my friend and father figure. He loved me genuinely and treated me like his own son. I have kept an old King James Bible he gifted me during my teenage years all these years. I learned spiritual disciplines from him, and he greatly helped me to develop a love for people, church, and missions.

"To become a good Bible student, you must keep a notebook," he advised. "Also, you need to memorize key Bible passages to help you minister to other people," he emphasized. I invited my cousin, Otchere, to join Bible studies with Brother Stephen. He baptized both of us the same day.

Brother Stephen set me up for preaching right away after conversion. He was an avid hospital and prisons minister. He spoke very little vernacular but preached boldly in English, which I tried to translate into our native Twi language. Asawasi is only a couple of miles away from the Manhyia Polyclinic. We were given permission to conduct morning worship services with the hospital's staff and patients. Twice every week, we arrived at the hospital around 5:30

a.m. to preach. Worship services lasted about thirty minutes. And we made friends with several of the hospital staff. Initially, I was a bit nervous preaching in public. But gradually, I became confident in leading songs, reading the Bible, and interpreting the devotional message in the open. Before he concluded, Brother Stephen always threw a challenge to the audience, stirring them up to pray and read the scriptures regularly. I still remember a couple of women who converted to be strong believers from the hospital ministry.

Brother Stephen was a member of the Asafo Church of Christ in Kumasi. Brother Ernest and a few young evangelicals started the Asafo church in 1976. Ernest was a product of the Ghana Bible College (GBC). Two American missionaries called Dewayne Davenport and Jerry Reynolds, in 1961, with financial support from the Cedars Church of Christ in Wilmington, Delaware, established the GBC. After their departure, Dr. Samuel B. Obeng became the principal of the college for more than three decades. Some of the founding members of the Asafo church were Stephen, Donkor, Clement, Baah, Tannor, Clement, Rachel, Abena, and Da Costa. At that time, there were only a handful of churches of Christ in Ghana. I was extremely nervous the first time I joined Brother Stephen to church. I had mixed feelings. I was glad to be among a group of passionate believers. At the same time, I was uncomfortable with their slow acapella worship service and classroom sanctuary. From childhood, I have been exposed to cathedral-type churches with beautiful compounds, pews, altars, paintings, melodious choirs, and powerful musical artifacts, including pipe organs.

What must be going on here? I asked myself. *If this were a true church of God, why are they so few? Also, why is there no choir? And why is the minister not properly dressed in a priestly garment like other churches?* These questions bothered me. "I don't think I like to come back here again. The church looks weird," I told Otchere.

"You are right," he said. "What we needed was proper baptism described in the Bible. I don't think we need to join a church where people sit on small wooden benches," he concluded. We went home disappointed.

Where we were raised in the Methodist tradition was very well organized and materially endowed. The demographics were multigenerational with older people, younger people, and children. In the city church, for instance, one could easily find several rich worshippers. There were many rich market traders, well-known professionals like teachers, lawyers, doctors, nurses, and civil servants. The music was great, and it was complemented by loud organ harmony. The priests were revered and well respected. They dressed in gorgeous priestly regalia. Beyond that, we worshipped in a beautifully painted imposing sanctuary with scarlet-and-white decorated interiors matched with cushioned pews. It was one of the best-known churches in town.

I was being trained as one of the young pianists, which came with little rewards like a paid summer job. I thought about all these things which made coming back to the new "miserable church" burdensome. I also kept thinking about the spiritual attractions at that poor little church. Their devotion to Bible study and spiritual disciplines was something I had never ever experienced before. The greatest of all was the thought of losing my newfound friendship with Evelyn. She was so special. Besides, I had become so used to Brother Stephen's love that I never wanted to miss him. Otchere came up with a plan.

"Let's maintain our membership at the Methodist church while we visit the evangelical church every once in a while."

"Brilliant idea," I said. For several weeks, that is what we did.

But Brother Stephen kept visiting us and stressed the need for continued fellowship. We were not bold enough to confess our concerns. One evening, when he came over to study the Bible with us, I plucked the courage to face him with our concerns about the misery we found associated with his little evangelical church.

"How could it be that the church of the living God will be so poor to maintain a tiny public-school classroom as sanctuary?" I questioned. "Also, why is your church not properly organized with priestly leadership, altar, choir, or piano?" I asked.

Brother Stephen's answer was gentle and succinct. "I have no church," he said. "In fact, no one can claim to have a church," he added. "The church belongs to God, and it was Jesus Christ our Lord who established it through the shedding of his blood on the cross of Calvary," he concluded. He went on his usual scriptural tangent.

> And I tell you that you are Peter and on this rock, I will build my church, and the gates of Hades *will not overcome it.* I will give you the keys of the kingdom of heaven; whatever you bind on earth will be bound in heaven, and whatever you loose on earth will be loosed in heaven. (Matthew 16:18–19)

> There is one body and one Spirit, just as you were called to one hope when you were called; one Lord, one faith, one baptism; one God and Father of all, who is over all and through all and in all. (Ephesians 4:4–6)

> For no one can lay any foundation other than the one already laid, which is Jesus Christ. If anyone builds on this foundation using gold, silver, costly stones, wood, hay or straw, their work will be shown for what it is, because the Day will bring it to light. It will be revealed with fire, and the fire will test the quality of each person's work. (1 Corinthians 3:11–13)

He proceeded to give a lengthy commentary on the scriptures, but what hit me like a ton of bricks was his concluding passage:

> But it was Solomon who built a house for him. However, the Most High does not live in houses made by human hands. As the prophet says:
> "Heaven is my throne, and the earth is my footstool. What kind of house will you build for me?" says the Lord.

"Or where will my resting place be?" (Acts 7:47–49)

And let us consider how we may spur one another on toward love and good deeds, not giving up meeting together, as some are in the habit of doing, but encouraging one another—and all the more as you see the Day approaching.

If we deliberately keep on sinning after we have received the knowledge of the truth, no sacrifice for sins is left, but only a fearful expectation of judgment and of raging fire that will consume the enemies of God. (Hebrews 10:24–27)

Hmmm! "The Most High God does not live in houses made by human hands."

But I had always learned that God Almighty lived in the temple in Jerusalem.

"That was the old dispensation, not now," Brother Stephen said. "In the current dispensation where Christ Jesus reigns as king, your human body is the temple of God, and it is through which you ought to honor God, not any beautifully decorated well-endowed church building," he concluded.

I spent several days thinking about these answers. Finally, I made up my mind to go back to the evangelical church.

My mother did not see me at church for weeks and got extremely agitated. The bishop, priests, choirmaster, and some of my friends were worried. Some gossiped that I had been deceived into joining a "Nigerian church," believing that the Church of Christ belonged to Brother Stephen. Some of my mother's friends convinced her that I had been indoctrinated to join a new religious sect whose leader was a Nigerian. That was the first time my mother ever expressed disgust and concern about my faith. And that was the first time I remember disrespecting her. When she suggested I must quit meeting with the new church, I flatly refused. That greatly infuriated her. She reprimanded me and complained my insubordination was becoming annoying. For several days, she felt uncharacteristically cold and unfriendly toward me. Aside from missing me at church personally, she was worried about three things. First, she was concerned that I was being misled and brainwashed by a fanatic Christian group. Second, her pride about my piano was quickly eroding. Third, she feared I might lose my summer job at my "ancestral church." She was only right about the third concern. The Church of Christ was no secret society, cult, or fanatic Christian group. It was part of God's kingdom, like other Christian groups. Beyond that, it was more focused on spiritual disciplines and the proclamation of the gospel of Lord Jesus Christ than I had ever been exposed to from childhood. My summer job was terminated starting a long persecution story. But considering the horrific accounts of religious persecutions in scripture and history, suffering such as mine was a mere chicken feed.

> We are hard pressed on every side, but not crushed; perplexed, but not in despair; persecuted, but not abandoned; struck down, but not destroyed. We always carry around in our body the death of Jesus, so that the life of Jesus may also be revealed in our body. For we who are alive are always being given over to death for Jesus' sake, so that his life may also be revealed in our mortal body. So then, death is at work in us, but life is at work in you.
>
> It is written: "I believed; therefore, I have spoken." Since we have that same spirit of faith, we also believe and therefore speak, because we know that the one who raised the Lord Jesus from the dead will also raise us with Jesus and present us with you to himself. All this is for your benefit, so that the grace that is reaching more and more people may cause thanksgiving to overflow to the glory of God.
>
> Therefore we do not lose heart. Though outwardly we are wasting away, yet inwardly

we are being renewed day by day. For our light
and momentary troubles are achieving for us an
eternal glory that far outweighs them all. So we
fix our eyes not on what is seen, but on what is
unseen, since what is seen is temporary, but what
is unseen is eternal. (2 Corinthians 4:8–18)

The persecution of new converts can be historically traced from
the first century of the Christian era to the present day. Christian
missionaries and converts have both been targets of persecution,
sometimes to the point of being martyred for their faith, ever since
the emergence of Christianity. Since the emergence of Christian
states in Late Antiquity, Christians have also been persecuted by
other Christians over differences in doctrine characterized as heresy.

But before all these, they shall lay their
hands on you, and persecute you, delivering you
up to the synagogues, and into prisons, being
brought before kings and rulers for my name's
sake. (Luke 21:12)

Early Christians were persecuted for their faith at the hands
of both the Jews, from whose Christianity arose, and the Romans
who controlled many of the lands across which early Christianity was
spread in the Roman Empire. Early in the fourth century, the empire's
official persecutions were ended by the Edict of Serdica and the practice of Christianity legalized by the Edict of Milan. Shortly thereafter,
Christians began persecuting each other. The schisms of late antiquity
and the Middle Ages—including the Rome-Constantinople schisms
and the many Christological controversies—together with the later
Protestant Reformation provoked severe conflicts between Christian
denominations. During these conflicts, the various denominations
frequently persecuted each other and caused sectarian violence.

In the twentieth century, Christian populations were persecuted, sometimes to the point of genocide, by various states, including the Ottoman Empire and its successor, which committed the

Hamidian massacres and Armenian genocide, the Assyrian genocide, and the Greek genocide, and officially atheist states such as the Soviet Union, Communist Albania, and North Korea.

Early Christianity began as a sect among Second Temple Jews, and according to the New Testament account, Pharisees, including Saul of Tarsus (prior to his conversion to Christianity as Paul), persecuted early Christians. The early Christians preached the second coming of a Messiah, which did not conform to their religious teachings. However, feeling that their beliefs were supported by Jewish scripture, Christians had been hopeful that their countrymen would accept their faith. Despite individual conversions, the vast majority of Judean Jews did not become Christians.

Claudia Setzer asserts that "Jews did not see Christians as clearly separate from their own community until at least the middle of the second century." Thus, acts of Jewish persecution of Christians fall within the boundaries of synagogue discipline and were so perceived by Jews acting and thinking as the established community. The Christians, on the other hand, saw themselves as persecuted rather than "disciplined."

Intercommunal dissension began almost immediately with the teachings of the outspoken Stephen at Jerusalem, who was considered an apostate by Jewish authorities. According to the Acts of the Apostles, a year after the Crucifixion of Jesus, Stephen was stoned for his alleged transgression of the faith, with Saul (later converted as Paul) acquiescing and looking on.

In AD 41, when Herod Agrippa, who already possessed the territory of Herod Antipas and Philip (his former colleagues in the Herodian Tetrarchy), obtained the title of King of the Jews, in a sense reforming the Kingdom of Judea of Herod the Great (r. 37–4 BC). Herod Agrippa was reportedly eager to endear himself to his Jewish subjects and continued the persecution in which James the Great lost his life, Peter the apostle narrowly escaped, and the rest of the apostles took flight.

After Agrippa's death in 44, the Roman procuratorship began (before 41, they were prefects in Iudaea Province). Those leaders maintained a neutral peace until the procurator Porcius Festus died in 62. After that, the high priest called Ananus ben Ananus took advantage of the power vacuum to attack the church and executed James the Just, one of the elders of the church in Jerusalem. The New Testament states that Paul was himself imprisoned on several occasions by the Roman authorities, stoned by the Pharisees and left for dead on one occasion and eventually taken to Rome as a prisoner. Peter and other early Christians were also imprisoned, beaten, and harassed. The first Jewish rebellion, spurred by the Roman killing of three thousand Jews, led to the destruction of Jerusalem in AD 70, the end of Second Temple Judaism (and the subsequent slow rise of Rabbinic Judaism), as well as the disempowerment of Jewish persecutors. According to an old church tradition, which is mostly doubted by historians, the early Christian community fled Jerusalem beforehand to the already pacified region of Pella.

Luke T. Johnson nuances the harsh portrayal of the Jews in the Gospels by contextualizing the polemics within the rhetoric of contemporaneous philosophical debate, showing how rival schools of thought routinely insulted and slandered their opponents. These attacks were formulaic and stereotyped, crafted to define who was the enemy in the debates but not used with the expectation that their insults and accusations would be taken literally, as they would be centuries later, resulting in millennia of anti-Semitism in Christianity.

In the fourth century, John Chrysostom argued that the Pharisees alone, not the Romans, were responsible for the murder of Jesus. However, according to Walter Laqueur, "absolving Pilate of guilt may have been connected to the missionary activities of early Christians in Rome and their desire not to antagonize those who they wanted to convert."

Although my mother never concealed her indignance about my leaving the Methodist church, she was still convinced about my integrity and ability to make good judgments concerning faith matters. My friends made a big deal about my church fervor. I became the subject of mockery whenever I resisted their invitation to disco clubs with girls. Then there was the problem with my summer job. I was terminated at the peak of military brutalities and famine in my country. I had mixed feelings whether or not I should return to my mother's church to win my job back. I needed to feed and clothe myself as a young adult.

But the summer job is already gone. There is no need crying over spilled milk, I said to myself. *I can only but trust God to survive*, I reflected soberly.

Knowing that I had no money, my stepmother became more vicious and emotionally abusive. My father became excessively dismissive of my personal needs. They cared little I was still a student. Something incredibly mysterious happened one Sunday at church. It was announced that a shipload of food, drinks, medicines, and clothing had arrived at Ghana's main harbor at Tema to be freely distributed to members of the churches.

The announcement came as if it was untrue. That was a huge relief. The entire assembly erupted in worship: "Hallelujah, hallelujah," "Praise the Lord, praise the Lord," "Amen and amen." So deafening were the shouts that some passersby peeped to see what was going on.

A few days later, convoys of large trucks loaded with all kinds of food started arriving at the Ghana Bible College (GBC) a few miles away. The GBC served as the main food distribution point for the northern part of Ghana. Otchere, my cousin, was appointed as one of the distribution supervisors. All churches of Christ members in Ghana received biweekly rations from early 1983 until about late 1984 at no cost whatsoever. The depots in Accra and Kumasi also distributed food to the poor, children, and several aged people. They distributed food and medicines to several public institutions including orphan homes, schools, and prisons. Evelyn, Otchere, and I became a source of food supply, which ultimately saved our families from famine. Because of the food, the churches of Christ in Ghana grew numerically like has never been seen in Africa.

The church at Asafo was not only important for my spiritual formation but also behavioral decency and leadership. Where I lived in the slums, temperate behavior and basic etiquette were almost missing in daily conversations. The young people and gangs shouted insults, cursed, and regularly fought in the streets. Our parents hardly thought us basic well-mannered expressions like "please," "I am sorry," "I beg your pardon," "you have a go first," and so on. It seemed like every young person was rude and impolite. The boys and girls yelled at each at the least provocation. At church, however, Brother Donkor (the minister) instructed lessons on good manners some of us so desperately needed. Preacher Donkor was highly educated and well-traveled. Aside from preaching, he kept an academic job at the prestigious University of Science and Technology. He was like a father to many young people in the church. We regularly went to his office or bungalow to receive counseling, share our fears and anxiety, pray, and learn from his wisdom. One of his major accomplishments was a special course to train young men in biblical studies, ministry, and leadership. I was a beneficiary. For more than three years, we met two hours every Sunday afternoon to pursue the course. Among others, we surveyed the Old and New Testaments, studied biblical theology and interpretation, preaching, and exegetical studies using Greek lexicons. We used Sunday evening worship services to prac-tice our teaching and preaching skills. Then he assigned groups of two or three to pursue outreach in the Abrotia, Asafo, Amakom, and Fante New Town townships. My first preaching assignment was nerve-racking. I was about twenty-one years old. Naturally, I opted to speak on the subject of "hope." I began by defining "hope" using scriptures from Hebrews 11:1. Next, I gave context to "hope" using the biblical story of Job, after which I drew parallels about my per-sonal difficulties and concluded with some words of encouragement that "Jesus is the answer to all hopelessness," citing Ecclesiastes 9:4; Psalm 25:3; Psalm 37:9; and Job 14:7–8.

> Mortals, born of woman, are of few days and full of trouble. They spring up like flowers and wither away; like fleeting shadows, they do not endure. Do you fix your eye on them? Will you bring them before you for judgment? Who can bring what is pure from the impure? No one! A person's days are determined; you have decreed the number of his months and have set limits he cannot exceed. So look away from him and let

him alone, till he has put in his time like a hired laborer. At least there is hope for a tree: If it is cut down, it will sprout again, and its new shoots will not fail. Its roots may grow old in the ground and its stump die in the soil, yet at the scent of water it will bud and put forth shoots like a plant. (Job 14:1–9)

As a student of the Bible, one subject I have had trouble understanding fully is church music. Churches of Christ generally use acapella music without instrumental accompaniment during worship services. This is contrary what I experienced as a boy raised in the Methodist church. As mentioned before, I sang in the choir and learned to play the piano when I was a teenager. This was not the case at the Asafo Church of Christ. Although I love acapella music, I was surprised why instruments were eliminated from church worship. Brother Stephen tried to explain to me using scripture. I have done extensive studies ever since, but admittedly, my understanding of the topic is still insufficient and possibly far from accurate. When Brothers Stephen and Evelyn came to visit me at home one evening, they saw me reading and translating music staff notation from the Methodist hymnal into tonic sol-fa, at which they were extremely impressed.

"Can you read music? And can you teach and lead songs at church?" Brother Stephen asked.

"Sure," I responded without thinking. After a few weeks, the minister appointed me as music director for the church. That revived my love for church music. Since then, I have taught hymns and led songs in more than a dozen different congregations.

6

African University

Today, there are more than 140 universities and colleges in Ghana. Thirty years ago, that was impossible. When I was in high school, Ghana's total population was about 16.7 million. At that time, there were only three universities in the country. How poor students like me managed to receive higher education remains a mystery.

While in sixth form (upper-tier high school), I met other students who, like me, had exceptional intellectual abilities but were beset with serious financial, social, and emotional problems. I remember one of my classmates (now a lawyer and politician) who struggled so badly that although he had free tuition, boarding, and lodging, still nearly dropped out of school because his parents could not afford to buy him basic school supplies like uniform, shoes, and writing implements. Thomas was too smart to drop out of school. The headmaster, therefore, decided to personally fund his needs. Financial constraints coupled with emotional stress badly affected my General Certificate of Examination Advanced Level (GCE A level) preparation and output. In West Africa, students who return poor grades at the regional examinations generally cannot go back to their school to retake the test. They can only do so in private capacity. This was one of the most difficult circumstances I ever faced. These were still the days of economic hardships, military dictatorships, and famine. There was no one I could turn to. There was no chance for me to find a summer job.

"My life is such a wreck," I complained to Adu, one of my friends.

"Just keep trying, Kwaku," he said. "We are all in the same boat. There is no way we can succeed in life without good education," he consoled me.

Unlike the US, there are no well-crafted standardized tests for university admission in West Africa outside scores reported by the West African Examinations Council (WAEC). As a result, the universities in Ghana are compelled to establish a cutoff passing grade for various undergraduate programs based on candidates' test scores. That notwithstanding, the universities hardly paid attention to their own admission requirements. The system was corrupt and extremely abused. I do not think much has changed now. Some students from affluent families and the political class were often favored. I remember one of my friends who failed an interview for selection into the medical school mainly because none of his family members was associated with the medical field. Yet this boy achieved one of the highest A-level grades during his year group. Students who achieved an aggregate score of six to fifteen were technically qualified to pursue degree courses. The grading scale was A–E, with aggregate six being the highest grade and fifteen the lowest. Due to intense competition for placement, there was no possibility for borderline admissions (i.e., aggregates thirteen to fifteen) unless the student had deep family or political connections or part of the university top brass. For science and engineering majors, the cutoff point was aggregate fifteen. It was impossible to gain admission into a science program with such an aggregate score. This applied to me, and my only chance was to rewrite the A-level examinations to better my grades.

"But how could I do this without my parents' help?" I soliloquized. "My mother has no money, and I have no job. O Lord God, please help me," I prayed. I requested Brother Frank and Evelyn to keep me in their prayers. Their response was positive.

Was I worried about access to university education? Surely I was. I have known from a very early age that in Africa, the success of poor boys and girls depended mainly on getting a good education. Although my mother had no formal education, she believed in this philosophy with absolute conviction. In truth, however, I was more concerned about poverty and hunger at that time than going to college. In Africa, our elders say, "He who has life has treasure. And no one knows what tomorrow may bring." Day after day, I walked miles away from home to find food at my sister's (Auntie B's) house at the opposite side of town.

I said to myself one day, *Is this trekking back and forth a useful thing at all? Maybe not*, I concluded. Oftentimes, I returned home hungrier than before, having walked hours under the tropical, sweltering sun.

One warm evening, a rich executive (a Muslim) who lived a few blocks away from my house recruited me as a private teacher for his children to improve their reading, writing, and numeracy skills. Despite the paltry wages he paid, I worked so hard as if my life depended on that job. Prior to that, Brother Stephen had taught me many lessons about hard work, ethics, and honesty. As a train driver, he took his job very seriously, working for the Ghana Railway Corporation. I still remember numerous conversations we had about his job. His work ethics were grounded on biblical principles, and he worked for his employers as if he were working for God (Colossians 3:22–25). Those lessons have been invaluable for me all these years.

> Slaves, obey your earthly masters in everything; and do it, not only when their eye is on you and to curry their favor, but with sincerity of heart and reverence for the Lord. Whatever you do, work at it with all your heart, as working for the Lord, not for human masters, since you know that you will receive an inheritance from the Lord as a reward. It is the Lord Christ you are serving. Anyone who does wrong will be repaid for their wrongs, and there is no favoritism. (Colossians 3:22–25)

When the man noticed some improvement in his children's reading and arithmetic, he found me a full-time job as a "pupil-teacher" at the private elementary school in downtown Kumasi where his kids attended. In most part of Africa where trained teachers are often in short supply, untrained teachers (i.e., pupil teachers) may be recruited to teach in schools with minimum in-service training. That job was heaven-sent. I did not only make enough money for my upkeep but I was also able to pay for my tuition and registration to rewrite the A-level examinations at the Kumasi Polytechnic. Today, Kumasi Polytechnic is a public technical university. Then, it was an advanced technical college mandated to train middle-level technicians at the higher national diploma (i.e., associate degree level).

That is where I met Dr. Nyamah, one of the best chemistry teachers I have ever known. Dr. Nyamah was a senior lecturer at the University of Science and Technology and an adjunct instructor at the Kumasi Polytechnic. He clearly inspired my love for chemistry. He was highly intelligent and exuded exceptional teaching skills in the classroom. His patience, teaching experience, and examination preparation skills were undoubtedly helpful. He explained chemistry concepts in a very succinct way and showed us simple ways to solve stoichiometry and other chemistry problems in a stepwise manner. His teaching style was exceedingly better than what I had experienced previously. When the WAEC published the next A-level results, my grades had improved significantly. I was selected into the bachelor's degree program at the University of Science and Technology. I went to look for Dr. Nyamah immediately after I arrived on campus on move-in day. He did not only inspire my interest in chemistry but also ignited my love for teaching the subject. The University of Science and Technology has now been renamed as the Kwame Nkrumah University of Science and Technology (KNUST). KNUST is one of the most prestigious academic institutions in Africa. Its focus on science and technology education and research is quite comparable to some of the major universities in Asia, Europe, and the US. I was assigned to the Independence Hall, popularly called INDECE Hall, as a dormitory resident. I met Akomeah at the porter's lodge on move-in day. Like me, Akomeah was at the porter's lodge to register as a freshman.

"My name is Stephen Opoku-Duah, and what is your name?" I asked.

"My name is Francis Kwame Akomeah," he replied.

"You look like a freshman, correct?" I inquired.

"Oh yeah, I am," he said. "Do you have an assigned roommate?" he asked.

"No, please!" I replied.

"Since you are a science major like me, can we room together?" he asked.

"Absolutely," I responded.

That is how Akomeah and I became best friends. Today, INDECE Hall is a mixed hall. That was not the case thirty years ago. It was then solely a male hall. The hall population was very low, probably less than six hundred students. Today, a couple of thousand students share the same facility. The nine-story annex hall was single occupancy generally allocated to seniors, students on medical rotations, and graduate students. The main hall was double occupancy. The "bridge" was probably the best-preferred wing at the main hall. That location was a priority for most returning students. Akomeah and I were allocated to room 16 in the east wing. I could never room with a better person than Akomeah. He was a calm young man with a feminine-like voice. He was slim, tall, and handsome-looking. He was polite and always neatly dressed. Although we were different personalities, we had lot of personal things in common. We both respected other people's opinions, maintained good hygiene and eating habits, and enjoyed humor, family, and cultural values. What was different were our Christian views and beliefs. Although Akomeah professed a member of the Sabbath Day Adventist Church from childhood, he had stopped attending church long before coming to college. Akomeah and I grew in love and respect for one another and became the best of friends. We studied hard and assisted one another with homework assignments and science projects. We had lots of fun like brothers. The fact that he was from Adansi Akokerri and I was from the Amansie District became another important bond of friendship. His hometown was just thirty miles away from where I was born. Because he had no relatives in Kumasi, he often felt homesick, for which reason I took him home at the least opportunity to eat home-cooked meals together.

Although I was a dorm resident, I still attended church in the downtown area two to three times every week. One day, I inquired whether Akomeah would join me to church. His answer was yes. After a couple of Sunday visits, he expressed interest in in-depth Bible study with one of our Bible class teachers called Brother Charles. Charles was very knowledgeable in the scriptures. He was eloquent, with a great sense of humor, and extremely fluent in English. He visited several weekends to study the Bible with us. Akomeah had many important questions about the creation story, morality, Old Testament law, Sabbath-keeping, predestination, premillennialism, rapture, fasting and prayer, and tithing. When we fully answered most of his questions, he requested to be baptized. Akomeah became my very first convert on campus.

Recall that the second military coup d'état by Flt. Lt. J. J. Rawlings happened in December 1981. This brought on huge political tensions in my country amid harsh economic reforms, coupled with droughts and famine. Ghanaian university students were at the forefront in fighting against the then military dictatorship. Although the students fully embraced Rawlings's first coup d'état in 1979, they hugely detested his overthrow of Dr. Hilla Limann's elected government. While they found legitimacy with his mutiny and execution of corrupt military leaders, they considered his disruption of Limann's Peoples' National Party administration grossly unnecessary. Several student agitations against Rawlings's military regime started at the University of Ghana in Accra in 1982, when I was a freshman. It slowly extended to the campuses of KNUST and the University of Cape Coast. The military head of state (often called Chairman Rawlings in answer to Eastern dictators) decided to visit the university campuses to explain the objectives of his Provisional National Defense Council (PNDC) revolution. Sometime in October 1982, he visited the KNUST campus to address the students at the University Great Hall (largest assembly hall on campus). The students caused so much commotion and rudely defied Rawlings, which immensely infuriated him.

Before long, the students embarked on a nationwide riot. Led by leaders like Botwe, Amoah-Larbi, Asaga, Gyan, and Abu-Bonsra, we went on an extensive protest march through the city of Kumasi to court public sympathy and support, designed to create disaffection against the PNDC military regime. The ultimate goal was to force Rawlings to hand over power to an elected government. That is what caused Rawlings to make one of his famous television speeches: "Hand over to whom?" The students presented a written petition to the then—Ashanti Regional Secretary called Dwomoh Kesse. Like his military boss, he responded angrily to the students' concerns. His subsequent reaction was rather catastrophic.

Mr. Kesse brought in armed workers and miners (supposedly in support of the military regime) from the Obuasi Goldfield Corporation (members of the Workers' Defense Committee) to penalize ("discipline") the rioting students at the KNUST campus. A fierce battle ensued between the students and the mineworkers at the University's Paa Joe Stadium. To date, no one knows the accurate number of fatalities from that confrontation. Because I could directly see nasty confrontations from INDECE Hall, I witnessed several casualties some of whom were wounded female students from Africa Hall (main female hall at the time). The next day, the political authorities announced closure of the university. They brought in police and military troops to enforce the closure. Days later, similar riots broke up in the University of Ghana and the University of Cape Coast. Before long, all the public universities were closed, causing a disruption of academic work. The closure lasted for more than one year. During that time, the military leaders embarked on a fierce exercise to hound the student leaders. Many of them fled to Europe and neighboring West African countries. That is when students like Kyereme Gyan (younger brother of Rtd. Major Boakye Gyan) were captured and assassinated. When we returned to campus in late 1983, the military regime decided to "punish" the students by removing their feeding subsidy even though the country was facing intense famine. Student meals were therefore reduced to once daily. The effect of this was incalculable. Some students died of famine, and others quit their academic programs. Aside from that, academic and research work was seriously stymied. Because of the closures, completion of all graduate, professional, and undergraduate programs were delayed for more than one year.

The post-rioting years brought relative peace for academic work to prevail. Akomeah and I worked hard to complete our freshman and sophomore years. We tried to expand our campus mission efforts. This connected us to a small group of believers who met weekly for Bible studies and prayers. Fortunately, religious groups in Ghanaian universities and colleges are not restricted to practice their faith on campus. Try as we did, our group never found a suitable meeting place. I devised a solution.

"If I were to run for office as a hall leader, I would be qualified for a single occupancy at the annex block," I said. "I could then turn the room into a meeting place for our Bible studies and prayer."

That was a good idea, but not without a price. It cost me money and time to run a pseudo-campaign to win a seat at the student government called the Junior Common Room (JCR) and Student Representative Council (SRC). Fortunately, friends like Anthonia, Akomeah, Akoto, Markus, and Yartey graciously supported my campaign. Eventually, I won a competitive election and assumed the role of the Independence Hall JCR secretary. As hall secretary, I was entitled to a furnished single room. I converted the same into a meeting place for our small church group. We met there every week until my degree program concluded. That group marked the beginning of the KNUST Church of Christ. Today, there are more than four hundred staff and students who attend the church every Sunday for worship services.

Studying abroad and exchange programs are a common part of diversity and academic experiential learning in universities around the globe. KNUST is no exception. The biggest problem in Africa is that most students come from poor homes that are incapable of financing study abroad programs. I still do not exactly remember why I decided to pursue an exchange program in Europe (in my senior year) knowing very well that I had no means of financing the trip. My application was successful, and I was selected to pursue my study abroad program in Belgium. I was excited yet extremely anxious how this was going to happen. Evelyn (my girlfriend) and I talked about this for several weeks.

"I will be praying for you," she said.

"Okay. But you know, I will never find money to travel to Europe. It is too expensive for anyone to pay for me," I replied.

"You may never know. God can fund your trip. The Bible says the heavens and the earth belong to God, and He is the source of all riches. You only have to trust him," she said with an assuring voice.

"Have you discussed your plans with Afreh, your friend?" she inquired.

"No," I retorted. "There is no way Afreh can afford to pay for me to travel to Belgium. He only owns a small engine-boring mechanical shop," I said.

She responded, "Just pray and speak to him about it. I think he will be glad to help you."

A few days later, I went to Afreh's shop to talk to him about my plans. He was shocked that had never appeared in our previous conversations.

"How much will it cost to travel to Belgium?" he inquired. "How much will the exchange program cost, and how would you pay for your stay there?" he probed.

"The exchange program itself is fully paid for by the International Association of Agriculture Students. My biggest problem is flight fare and a little travel money," I replied.

"So what is the cost of a year's return ticket to Belgium?" he inquired.

"I am not sure. I will have to find out," I replied.

"Please find out and let me know. I will be happy to pay for that," he said.

I was speechless! It took me a long time for all this to sink in. I made inquiries at a travel agency the following day. The return ticket was about $960 by local currency conversion. I reported my findings to Afreh. A couple of days later, he cut me a check nearly twice the amount of money I needed. I hurried to tell Evelyn what new miracle God had done.

"What did I tell you?" she asked. "We walk by faith, not by sight," she added.

"That is absolutely true. God help my unbelief!" I exclaimed.

When I told my mother I was traveling to Europe on a study abroad program after my last university examinations, she thought I was probably hallucinating or unhinged.

"How will you be able to do that? Your sister and I could not even find money to support your college education in Ghana. How do you think we could do so in Europe?" she asked with a stern, inquisitive demeanor.

It took me a long time to explain everything to her. Trying to explain higher education matters to my mother was like walking uphill backward or hauling water with a perforated bucket. The student exchange program was a great learning and cultural experience. Later, it opened doors of opportunity for me, including a research assistant job back home and graduate education in the Netherlands and Great Britain. After nearly two years in Europe, I returned to Ghana to complete my national service. As part of payback for free university education in Ghana, all college graduates are required to complete a one-year mandatory national service (National Service Act 426 of 1980). Through the above service, graduates are required to serve various sectors of the national economy including security services, health, education, agriculture, and social services. These graduate personnel are not paid wages but a stipend to help with food and transport. Unfortunately, I returned home when the service had been extended from one to two years, resulting from a backlog of applicants carried over from university program disruptions. Working my national service in Accra presented enormous challenges. I had just started a family. Taking care of a young family without a full-time job was no mean responsibility. The worst part was that the government found it hard to pay our meager monthly stipend worth $25 on a regular basis. I turned myself into a nighttime cab driver to generate extra income.

Unlike in the US, cabs are not metered in most parts of Africa. There are only a few taxi companies. The cab business remains in the hands of individuals often registered as cooperatives. The Nkrumah

Circle—Adabraka Taxi Drivers' Union is a good example. Aside from the unions, there are several independent cab drivers without assigned routes, called "floating drivers." I joined the floating drivers' group in Accra. A highly successful day's job is when passengers ride what is in Ghana's local parlance as "chartered taxi" or "dropping trips." In a "chartered trip," the rider bargains his or her fare for every specific trip. This is usually gainful to the cabdriver for two reasons. The driver does not unnecessarily lose travel time while saving on gasoline at the same time. Fate was unkind to me one warm evening. Two young women, probably in their late twenties or early thirties "chartered" my cab and bargained a handsome compensation from about 4:30 p.m. until about 10:30 p.m. That was big fish. After running several errands, they asked me to drop them at the Hotel President at Adabraka. Downtown Adabraka has some of the best and most popular entertainment spots in Accra. The women requested me to wait in the parking lot while they said goodbye to some friends they purportedly had been hosting in the hotel. After that, I was to take them home. We arrived at the hotel at about 9:00 p.m. When they failed to show up after more than one hour, I got curious and inquired about them at the front desk. To my horror, they had escaped from the back door without paying me a penny.

"Are you a professional taxi driver?" the front desk attendant asked.

"No, a part-time driver," I answered. She burst into laughter. "Why? What is wrong? Is there a problem?" I queried.

"No, but those ladies you call customers have no associations here. They are hookers and swindlers," she said. "They have escaped from the back door. They have swindled many taxi drivers like you," she said.

"So why don't you cause their arrest?" I protested.

"Sorry, man. It is not our job," she said. "Next time, please remember to take payment before serving chartered trips. That is what all professional taxi drivers do," she advised.

I arrived home late, tired, and dejected.

"I am devastated," I said to Evelyn.

"What's the problem? Are you okay?" she asked.

I told her all that has transpired and how I have been badly swindled by hookers.

"You don't have to be dejected. You acted foolishly. How could you give a free ride your entire night to call girls in a con place like Accra?" she yelled with rage. Evelyn's reaction augmented my humiliation. She was right. We did not even have money for baby food that day.

Finding a job after national service was a nightmare. In many developing economies, governments remain the largest employer for new university graduates. The private sector is severely emaciated. The economy at that time in Ghana was in tatters. The Rawlings administration was under intense pressure from the World Bank and International Monetary Fund to pursue a Structural Adjustment Program to help return the economy to sound health. One of the principal requirements was public sector reforms, which demanded a reduction of government spending, downsizing the bloated civil service, and a three-year moratorium on public sector employment. Finding a job was like beating the thigh of the elephant with pebbles.

Both my wife and I had no regular income for two years. Evelyn decided to pursue dressmaking apprenticeship while I continued with my taxi job. We kept praying and trusting God for another miracle. While reading the daily newspaper one weekend, I saw a job advertisement seeking for a water science research assistant at the Council for Scientific and Industrial Research (CSIR). Analogous to public universities, the CSIR is the largest science and technology research institution in Ghana. CSIR employment is some of the highest paying jobs in the country. The application process was tedious and time-consuming. In addition, it demanded extreme thoroughness. I had no prior job experience in Ghana, but I had good work ethics from my short period in Belgium. I completed the application documents and handed them in before the application deadline. Evelyn and I fasted and prayed for God's help. I knew nothing about the CSIR or the core responsibilities of the vacant position except the scanty information displayed in the advertisement. I was certain there were going to be large number of applicants. I knew several colleagues who, like me, had been searching for jobs without much success. I could not go to sleep that night. I rolled over several times in my bed, with thoughts about competition for the job intensely on my mind. Still, I trusted in God's favor. A few weeks later, I had a letter inviting me to interview for the job. This was a group interview. Just as I predicted, there were multiple applicants, some of whom I knew very well from my former university. In fact, three of them were colleagues from my graduating class, all of them very smart people. Those were the days of no mobile phones. Pay phones were even hard to find in a city like Accra except at the central post office. After waiting for three weeks without response from the CSIR human resources (HR) department, I personally called their offices to inquire about the status of my application. To my utter disappointment, I failed to land the job.

"I am shattered. I did not get the job," I reported sadly to Evelyn when I returned home.

"Oh no, that's so terrible," she exclaimed. "But do you know what? God's time is the best," she said softly. "When the right time comes, you will get a job, and you will get one of the best jobs," she assured.

She wrapped her hands around my neck, kissed my forehead, and tried to console me while tears rolled down my cheeks.

That was one of the saddest days of my life. I could not understand why God would refuse me a job I so badly needed. The memories of the CSIR laboratories and their well-furnished offices kept rolling back to me like a monk in a trance. I kept wondering what I did wrong at the interview anytime I drove past the CSIR campuses at the plush airport district. Instinctively, however, I strongly believed I would one day find a job in academia. If not the CSIR, then one of the public universities. A couple of weeks later, I had an unusually large mail package from CSIR. My mails passed through the Nsawam Road Church of Christ office. When I received the package, I started shaking as if I have received some terrible news. I simply could not open the package. I could not wait for the evening Bible class to conclude. I drove home and showed Evelyn the package, feeling so hysterical.

"Open it. What is it?" she screamed.

"Praise God! I have been offered the job!" I exclaimed.

"You are probably dreaming," she said.

"No, I am not. See the appointment letter." I handed her the paper.

We burst into worshipping and praising God.

Our little daughter was a bit frightened and unsure of what was happening when she saw us jumping about and praising God. She probably thought we were out of our minds.

I hardly caught any sleep that night. *Is this package wrongly addressed to me or what?* I kept thinking. Then I quickly remembered what the apostle Paul says in the scriptures:

> And we know that all things work together
> for good to those who love God, to those who are
> called according to His purpose. (Romans 8:28)

Another miracle has occurred. I wanted this job so badly, but I was denied. I brooded over for several days, consoled myself, and decided to move on. Then a few weeks later, I was offered the same job under unbelievable circumstances. Later, I discovered that the position was offered not because I was the most qualified or experienced applicant but because the selected candidate declined the offer after he tried unsuccessfully to find accommodation in town. The HR department, therefore, determined I was the second most qualified applicant and offered me the position. That is how little steps of faith landed my first professional science job. A rookie scientist emerged on the scene.

7

Rookie Scientist

Like many places in Africa, career counseling at high school or college was zero during my studentship. Career counseling, job fairs, internships, and field studies are recent invention in Ghana. In the past, it was students from wealthy families and those closely acquainted with academics or professionals who often benefitted from career coaching. I was never in this category of students. I had to figure out my future career by asking some of my teachers to help me decide. Intuitively, two types of careers appealed to me. I wanted to work in a bank or financial institution or as a college professor. I did not know any banker, but I knew professors like Dr. Nyamah whose middle-class lifestyle looked quite appealing. Many of the university professors (lecturers) I knew in Ghana dressed smartly, drove in nice cars, lived in well-furnished bungalows provided by the universities, and their children attended some of the best high schools in the country. One of the most popular beliefs in Africa is that bank managers are extremely rich. Whether that was the case, I was not exactly sure.

After college, I applied for a few banking jobs without success. My degree in science was probably the least considered for banking jobs. The closest I came was an assistant manager's position at a publicly owned commercial bank in Accra. Because banking jobs are perceived to be lucrative, vacant positions are hardly advertised in

Ghana. The popular rumor was that bank professionals and recruiters secretly employed their family members, cronies, and applicants who could afford bribes. One evening, my friend's wife, Priscilla, took me to speak with her uncle who was the bank's area manager about a vacant position. I was asked to complete application documents, followed by a couple of interviews at their HR office. Evelyn and I prayed for God's intervention. Because I could not afford a bribe, the position was filled behind my back. I knew God did not want me to become a banker. I believed he wanted me to do something completely different. That was how my search for an academic position began.

My job as a laboratory research assistant was quite challenging. The chief scientist and director of institute (Nii Ayibotele) demanded a lot from his staff. He was a class-act civil engineer and hydrologist. He trained several young scientists to teach, research, and execute consultancy jobs. Aside from analytical skills and problem-solving, he emphasized soft skills including science publishing, oral presentation, teamwork, financial accounting, and project management. In Ghana, personal computers in the early 1990s were quite rare at public workplaces including universities and research institutes. Nii Ayibotele was ahead of many industry leaders in the country. He conducted extensive searches for state-of-the-art hardware and software academic packages and created an aggressive program for computer applications in all aspects of hydrological, hydrogeological, and water chemistry education and research. He hired computing consultants to train his staff in key software applications including word processing (WordPerfect), spreadsheet (Lotus 123), databases (dBase-4), and coding (Fortran-90). This enabled the scientists to complete large-scale projects in digital formats which, hitherto, were painstakingly done by cartographers. For the first time in the history of Ghana, a national hydrogeological map at the scale of 1:250,000 was produced. Some of the water and environmental engineers employed computed aided design (CAD) software to create new water and wastewater treatment systems while rookies like me helped to process and analyze large datasets generated from nationwide automatic weather and gauging stations and water quality data across large river basins including the Volta River system. Computerization enabled us to complete several national projects funded by the World Bank, UNESCO, UK's Department for International Development, USAID, and Danish International Development Agency. Although exciting, my job demanded extensive travel across the country, which put a strain on my spouse because we had two little girls to take care of. At the same time, Evelyn was developing a well-paid career in dressmaking and training a dozen apprentices. Thankfully, my mother-in-law arrived from Nigeria to help take care of our children.

One day, I was called to the director's office.

"You are learning fast and doing well on the job," he said. "I think it is time for you to pursue graduate studies abroad," he added.

My heart began to beat very fast.

"How can I do that, sir?" I asked.

"Just like your supervisor, I will endorse your application for the Netherlands Fellowship Program through the Ministry of Finance," he added. "You will be awarded a full graduate fellowship for two years, and you will be entitled to study leave with pay. You must check with the HR office to begin the application process immediately," he concluded.

I just could not believe what had happened when I left my boss's office. I praised God and said to myself: "Thank you, Lord. My academic and research career is now on a great footing."

The scholarship process was quite complicated. It took nearly six months to complete. Finally, I left for the Netherlands to commence a master's degree in water chemistry at the prestigious Wageningen University & Research. Wageningen is Netherland's topmost university and ranked fifty-ninth among the world's best universities in academic and research excellence. A few months later, Evelyn joined me at Wageningen. The Netherlands (which means the lowlands) is a beautiful little country whose culture is deeply rooted in its history and landscape.

Historically, Dutch culture and democracy is one of the most liberal systems on the planet. That required a believer and immigrant like me to exercise self-control to effectively deal with bombarding sensuality. The good part is that their culture of self-organization and reception to cultural diversity is unmatched in Europe. Nearly everyone in Holland, from children to elderly people, carries a pocket diary in order not to miss appointments. Dutch people get extremely agitated when their train is late for two minutes. Keeping organized is one of my biggest cultural lessons from Holland. The culture of bicycles and dikes is strongly linked with the Dutch landscape. Nearly 30 percent of the country lies below sea level, and that explains the numerous dikes in the country. Bicycles remain the most common means of transport. Their capital city, Amsterdam, has so many water-filled canals that it has been described as the "Venice of Northern Europe." The Dutch society have some of the best water engineers in the world. Nearly 50 percent of their terrestrial landscape has been reclaimed from the sea. There is a common saying that "God created the earth, but the Dutch created Holland." Evelyn and I had a wonderful two-year stay in the Netherlands. We made some very good friends including Marlese and Sytze, and Anneke and Rob. Dutch people are some of the friendliest peoples on planet earth.

Wageningen University has some of the most rigorous graduate programs in the world, most of them offered in English. Their graduate water engineering and chemistry program gave me a solid foundation as a practicing scientist and academic. The best part of the program was its emphasis on field experiential learning, computational analysis, and development of soft skills. We completed field studies in Belgium, Luxembourg, France, Spain, and the Czech Republic. In my final year, my class spent twelve weeks in southern Spain to study wetland pollution and desiccation of the Guadalupe River basin using remote sensing technology. Twenty-eight students and six professors (from nine countries) participated in this study.

Something bizarre happened after our second week in Spain. Some of the students invited their girlfriends to spend the night in the male dormitory, against university rules. Serious confrontations arose among the students, which threatened to disrupt the academic exercise. To diffuse the problem, I created a political structure analogous to an African chieftaincy to engender respect and discipline. Our professors knew nothing about the problems and my planned solution. The students agreed for me to be the chief. I selected two advisers, one male and one female. We created a miniature legislature and judiciary supported by a three-man police force. The legislature quickly drew up dorm regulations to guide behavioral ethics. Students who violated the rules were tried by the judiciary and sanctioned by paying a fine, which was used to purchase drinks and snacks. The system worked perfectly. My role opened the door to discuss culture, ethics, and scriptures with some students. Ultimately, this became known to the university administration, and that won me the Vice Chancellor's Leadership Award during graduation.

Disaster struck when I returned from Spain. While working in the laboratory one Monday evening, Evelyn called me to hurry back home with an anxious tone. I felt a bit panicky. I got onto my bicycle and galloped home like a horse. When I pressed for a reason, she simply ignored me.

"Are you okay, Yaa? Is there any problem? Are you sick or hurt? Do I need to call the police?" I asked.

"No! Please come home immediately. I need to you check something quickly," she pleaded.

I kept wondering what the matter was. I just obliged.

Evelyn looked worried when I got home. Still, she refused to explain the reason for summoning me home unless I had a shower and finished my dinner. I knew something was wrong!

"Your instructions are simply unusual and weird," I said. "Please tell me what has happened, and let me apologize if I have done something wrong," I pleaded.

When she finally saw weariness in my eyes, she broke the news that she received a call from Ghana that my mother passed away the previous day from a massive stroke. I could hardly control my emotions. I wept uncontrollably. My mother was everything to me. I loved her immensely. She loved me exceedingly. Out of poverty, she did all she could to see me become a successful person. Repeatedly she told me, "The only way you will succeed as a man and overcome poverty is to focus on church, study hard, and be self-controlled." Sadly, she did not live long enough to see me fulfill this dream. Fortunately, she saw me travel that road before departing. A couple of weeks later,

Evelyn and I traveled back to Ghana for her funeral. That was a huge psychological closure to our wonderful relationship as mother and son. Several years have passed, but I still miss her greatly! How I wish she knew my improbable career as a science professor in the US.

We had a wonderful time in Holland but still missed our church family. We started visiting the Dutch Reformed Church (similar to Presbyterian Church). We loved going there, but we later stopped attending because of their continued use of the Dutch language for the liturgy. The Dutch Reformed Church was the largest Christian denomination in the Netherlands from the Protestant Reformation in the Middle Ages until 1930. It was the foremost Protestant denomination and, since 1892, one of the two major reformed denominations along with the Reformed Church in the Netherlands. It was the church of the Dutch royal family until it merged into the Protestant Church in the Netherlands, a united church of both Reformed and Evangelical Lutheran theological traditions. The allegiance to the Dutch Reformed Church was a common feature among Dutch immigrant communities and became a crucial part of Afrikaner nationalism in South Africa. John Calvin shaped the theology of the Dutch Reformed Church around 1571. This happened through various theological developments and controversies during its history and several splits in the nineteenth century that greatly diversified Dutch Calvinism. The church functioned until 2004, then merged with the Reformed Churches in the Netherlands and the Evangelical Lutheran Church in the Kingdom of the Netherlands to form the Protestant Church. At the time of the merger, the Church had two million members organized in 1,350 congregations.

Eventually, we found the closest church of Christ at Driebergen, a little town nearly thirty-two miles north of Wageningen. There were only thirty-five members. Still, they had a vibrant English worship service and Bible class. The minister, Brother Henk, was married to an American woman from a family of missionary workers. We made friends there in a very short time. One day, Henk gave me the telephone number of an African family who previously called from Amsterdam to the church office. Amazingly, that was a family we knew quite well back home in Ghana. That was Kwasi, his wife, Theresa, and their two little girls. When we finally met them, they introduced us to a Dutch family who were struggling to start a church at their residence. Evelyn and I immediately knew the Lord was opening a new door for mission work. We responded to the gospel call. We spent more than a year preaching and studying with several immigrant families who were yearning for the gospel of Christ. Soon, eight souls were baptized, which marked the starting point of the church of Christ in Amsterdam. Today, there are two large congregations in the city, made up of African immigrants and Dutch families. The work in Amsterdam has also opened doors for other immigrants to revive many dying churches in Europe. As of 2019, there were about thirty-seven immigrant churches of Christ in sixteen European countries.

I returned to my job in Ghana and got promoted as a water scientist in 1996. My job functions changed with more responsibility as a researcher and lecturer. I served on many important national science committees including the Volta-TIGER project funded by European Space Agency and UNESCO. My involvement in the river and near-ocean studies demanded travels across Africa and Europe, including eleven African countries and sixteen European countries. Some of the projects required long-term research fellowships, including a three-month residency at the International Center for Theoretical Physics (ICTP) at Trieste, Italy, a two-month stay at the Volta Basin Research Center at the University of Bonn, Germany, and a nine-month residency at the European Space Agency (ESA) at Frascati, Italy. My competence in water chemistry and remote sensing technology advanced tremendously. This came with a big cost. Some of my colleagues ganged up against me out of sheer envy. Many of them talked nicely when I was present but said bitter things behind my back. My supervisor, for instance, denied me good recommendations a couple of times. I became despondent and felt like quitting the job. I was getting more and more depressed. I kept things to myself. But Evelyn started to notice my unhappiness and questioned my mood.

"I know your job is busy and makes you travel frequently, but that comes with blessings for you and us. Why are you not happy? What is going on?" she asked.

"You are right, Yaa. Some of my colleagues make me very unhappy. They hate me because of my role in the European research projects. They think I am a stumbling block," I said. "You need to pray for me," I requested.

Evelyn and I prayed many times about my workplace difficulties. We prayed for all those who ganged up against me.

Two opportunities suddenly presented. In the first case, the elders of my local congregation approached me to consider the position of associate minister. Nsawam Road Church of Christ, located near the Kwame Nkrumah Interchange in Accra, is one of the largest acapella churches in Africa, with a membership of nearly 1,500. I jumped at the opportunity. Around the same time, our third child, Immanuel, was born. The joy of Kofi's birth and the church work brought tremendous relief for me to focus more on God than myself. In the second opportunity, I secured a British Commonwealth Scholarship to pursue doctoral studies in England. My young family arrived at Durham University at the beginning of the new millennium.

Like my two previous alma maters, Durham is one of the world's leading universities. As shown by the World Top 100 positions in the QS World University Rankings for 2021, it ranked eighty-sixth. A record of nineteen Durham subjects are in the World Top 100 of the QS World University Rankings by Subject 2020, including eleven in the World Top 50. Three of their subjects are in the World Top 10. Those are Theology and Religion (fourth), Archaeology (fourth), and Geography (tenth). In the *Times Higher Education* (*THE*) World University Rankings by Subject, five of Durham's subjects are ranked in the Top 100 including two in the Top 50 (Law and Arts and Humanities). In the *THE*'s Impact Rankings for 2020, Durham is in the world Top 50 for their contribution to four of the United Nations' Sustainable Development Goals (SDGs). It is also part of the world's Top 100 for a further seven SDGs. Nationally, Durham is consistently a top 10 UK university and ranked fourth in the Guardian University Guide 2021, seventh in the Complete University Guide 2021 and sixth in the *Times* and *Sunday Times* Good University Guide 2021. The rankings signal the university's excellence in teaching and research, combined with their all-round student experience.

This makes Durham's graduates highly sought after by employers around the world. Recently, Professor Stuart Corbridge, vice-chancellor and warden of Durham University, had this to say:

> Durham is one of the world's great universities and one of the most distinctive. We aim to inspire our students and staff to achieve extraordinary things and I am delighted that this is recognized by our continued high standing in global and national league tables.

Durham's research spans the world and beyond. Their physicists are currently using supercomputer simulations to test alternatives to Einstein's theory of general relativity while their archaeologists recently led the first UK university team ever to be permitted to undertake excavations within Beijing's Forbidden City. Durham also works with partners to encourage scholars from across the world to visit Durham and study the county's outstanding special collections. In March 2019, this led to the discovery of an eight-hundred-year-old royal charter from the reign of King John.

Durham itself is a historic ancient city in England. Monks from the Diocese of Lindisfarne around AD 995 built it. The Durham Cathedral and its adjacent castle are nearly one thousand years old. While the castle served as residence of the Bishop of Durham, the cathedral served the sanctuary needs and shrine containing the mortal remains of one of the most venerated Christian leaders called Saint Cuthbert, the bishop of Lindisfarne. Both edifices are designated UNESCO heritage sites and currently form part of the historical monuments of Durham University.

The Durham PhD program is one of the most rigorous research programs in the world. It follows the unique four-year advanced British degree model, which depends entirely on independent research without coursework. I spent the first six months completing a well-researched study proposal that was presented at a mini viva at the Department of Geography. Professors Tim P. Burt and Daniel Donoghue advised the research. The desktop, fieldwork, and laboratory work took three years while the last six months were used to produce a 395-page thesis titled: "Remote sensing of energy and water fluxes over Volta Savannah Catchments in West Africa." A three-man expert team chaired by Prof. Stuart Lane examined the thesis. I was the only African graduate in my class of 2007 and received an honorable mention. Prior to graduation, I taught undergraduate courses under the supervision of Prof. Daniel Donoghue, who generously allowed me to complete additional two years of post-doctoral fellowship working on two European Union research projects: (1) Volta-Tiger Project (ESA), and (2) "Characterization of the distribution, fate, and effects of industrial heavy metals in the Tees estuary in North East England." Up to this point, I had developed enough competence as a career university teacher and scientist. I was no longer a rookie!

8

Career Abroad

Not once, my European and American friends asked me, "Do you still have family living in Ghana?" "How often do you go to your home country?" "Don't you feel homesick?" "Are you going to retire in Ghana?" Also, many times has my bosom friend, K. B., asked me when I would be returning home. Some time ago, he asked, "You have stayed abroad for a long time, are you not tired being so far away from home? Why not think about coming back home?" Of course, I miss home. I miss my family. I miss my boyhood friends. I miss the village where I was born, and especially Kumasi where I grew up. There is no better place like home. Do you know something? I left Ghana to develop my career and pursue a good life for my family and myself. One of the most important reasons why I left my country was because I was pushed away by sheer envy and selfishness suffered at the hands of some of my working colleagues. I know a few Ghanaian professionals who have perished because of workplace envy and hatred. Africans know how to eliminate their competitors through demonic attacks. Not that I was scared to die, but I hated the consequences of my departure—insecurity of my young family. Second, the African society is endemically corrupt, superintended over by the political class and their business cronies. This has significantly erased any economic comfort due to the middle class. Those significantly impacted by the corrupt system are salaried professionals, including academics, scientists, doctors, teachers, and nurses. That partly explains why brain drain has notoriously infected the socioeconomic torso of sub-Saharan Africa. A UN/OECD World Migration Report (2013) has shown that nearly three million African professionals live and work in Europe, North America, Australia, and the Middle East, representing a nearly 50 percent increase over the previous decade, and much greater than any other region in the world. Considering my own experience, migration of African professionals to richer countries is not only for economic reasons, but personal security is also an important reason. I know some college friends who have lived outside Ghana since their youth not because they wanted to parasite Western economic prosperity but because they were forced to escape political tyranny from previous military juntas.

I was not ignorant about the value of my skill set in Ghana. Yet I was also aware of how much better I could serve my country while working abroad than at home. Over the past twenty-five years, I have found this thinking to be accurate. I have impacted water research, higher education, and rural development than I would have otherwise achieved back in Ghana. Let us consider a few specific examples here: (1) I have mentored and assisted eleven students to complete graduate and undergraduate studies in the UK, South Africa, and USA; (2) I have created strong academic partnerships between Ghanaian and US universities through the Carnegie-African Diaspora Fellowship Program; (3) I have published widely on the hydrology and water resources of the Volta River Basin; and (4) I have designed, tested, and installed new water-purification technologies to benefit distressed communities in four villages in the Ashanti Region. The practice of science in Africa is not easy. A few years ago, I successfully wrote a European Space Agency grant to establish a remote sensing laboratory at the Council for Scientific and Industrial Research, the foremost public research agency in Ghana. The purpose was to measure regional-scale energy and water fluxes driving the pollution, sedimentation, and desiccation of the White Volta Basin in West Africa. The project was abolished and the equipment dispersed by an envious, overbearing supervisor. There is nothing as stressful for a carpenter than having to produce a set of living room furniture without a saw, hammer, and chisel. Why my supervisor despised my research activities was not because he found no value for it but because he perceived the success of a young scientist as becoming unnecessarily powerful than his superiors. This is one of the reasons why Africa has paced far behind the world's economy. Many media and political commentators believe that poverty in sub-Saharan Africa is tied to the unhinged political leadership on the continent. That is certainly a fact. Africa's poverty is notoriously linked with greed, superstition, and antiquated traditions. In Ghana, for example, numerous traditional concepts and sayings are rooted in corruption. Take for example the following traditional sayings: "He who prepares aromatic food additives must never be prevented from licking their fingers" and "He who climbs to the top must never forget to bring some treasure home." I remember a story about one of my relatives when I was a little boy. The Akan tradition knows no cousins, so one of my mother's cousins was considered my uncle. He returned from the UK with a law degree from Oxford University and found a job at the legal department of the Ghana Cocoa Board. He quickly rose through the ranks to head the legal department and later, one of the deputy chief executive officers. Arguably, he was the most prominent person ever to have risen to the top from the village. He never brought home wealth, booty, or built a luxury house. Everyone thought he was silly and most ungenerous. The village was filled with rumors that he was the only executive in the superrich cocoa industry to have not enriched himself because of parsimony. Many of his colleagues were extremely wealthy because of their position. Suddenly, Rawlings's military junta commenced a no-nonsense auditing program of Ghana's top public servants. Although my uncle escaped to Nigeria for fear of his life, he was only one of such executives who safely returned to his country because of his honesty and incorruptibility. Some of his close colleagues were either executed by the military regime or died in exile because of corruption cases against them.

My contract at Durham University was close to ending by mid-2008. The hope for a teaching position in another university was getting slim. Evelyn and I started to commit this to God in prayer along with our kids. Some weeks later, we learned about an impending Bible seminar at church. The seminar presenter was Dr. Mike Moss, the then—Dean of Bible and Behavioral Sciences at the Ohio Valley University in the US. The seminar was hosted by the Newcastle upon Tyne Church of Christ with a topic on Christian leadership based on Paul's pastoral letters to the early church. How coincidental? At the same time, I was teaching Sunday Bible classes from 1 and 2 Timothy at our local Washington Columbia Church of Christ. Evelyn and I signed up to participate in the seminar. Dr. Moss is a class act American missionary, theologian, Bible professor, and author. He is a gifted public speaker too. He has authored several biblical books and commentaries and published extensively in various academic journals. Additionally, he has presented Bible seminars and workshops at many different universities and churches around the globe. His missionary travels have taken him to Palestine, Eastern and Central Europe, and Asia and converted many souls to Christ. His presentations at the Newcastle were superb. That was the first time I had listened to him. He was extremely captivating. I purchased a copy of his commentary on 1 and 2 Timothy and Titus. He detected my African accent immediately.

"You speak like a student I taught and supervised his research thesis. What is your name, and where do you come from?" he asked.

"My name is Steve, and I come from Ghana," I replied.

"Oh yeah? My former student was also from Ghana. His name is Augustine Tawiah," he said.

"How ridiculous! Augustine is my friend. I have known him since our high school days," I said.

"Where is he now? I have not heard from him since," he inquired.

"Back home in Ghana, working as the president of the Ghana Bible College," I replied.

"Great!" he exclaimed. "But what brought you to England, if I may ask?" he queried.

"I completed my PhD at Durham University and just about concluding a two-year postdoctoral research and teaching fellowship," I said.

"Excellent. In what discipline?" he asked.

"My background is water chemistry," I replied.

"No way. You must be kidding me," he exclaimed.

"Yes, that is true. He is not kidding," Evelyn interjected.

"We need you to come to the USA to teach at the Ohio Valley University," he said. "We have a vacant position for chemistry professor we have not filled for more than a year now. Would you be interested?" he asked.

"Well, I don't know," I said. "I need to check into it later," I concluded.

Dr. Moss gave me his business card and the telephone number of Dr. Jim Bullock, the provost of Ohio Valley University (OVU). He pleaded for me to get in touch as quickly as possible. When I brought up the OVU opportunity when driving home, Evelyn immediately dismissed it. She surmised it was going to be too difficult to pursue that appointment having previously migrated from Ghana and being quite well settled in the UK with our young family. She was right. Foreign migration is not an easy matter. The stresses of moving homes, travel, foreign culture, food, health issues, children and school matters, new job, communication barriers, family back home, settlement, and cultural integration are all too extremely difficult problems to fix. We moved to England when our two girls were in elementary school and our son was a toddler. By 2008, our girls were finishing high school, and our son, Immanuel, was a third grader. Evelyn's caution seemed plausible. I decided to shelve the idea.

"I will rather pursue a teaching or research career here in Great Britain than USA. It is much easier," I concluded.

"That's a good idea," said Evelyn.

I put Dr. Moss's business card in my office drawer and decided to ignore contacting the OVU provost. I kept thinking about something Mike Moss said when we first met.

"OVU is a Christ-centered academic community seeking to transform the lives of students," he said. "OVU is not just a college, it is also a mission field," he added.

"I have been in missions since I first truly believed. This is something I can identify with and would seriously like to be part of," I said confidently.

Later, I picked up a phone and called Dr. Bullock. "I was expecting your call," he said. "Dr. Moss spoke about you, and I would appreciate it if you could email me your resumé and go to our website to complete an application package," he added.

I sent him my resumé and deferred the application process until the next day.

I discussed my contact with Dr. Bullock with Evelyn when I got home. I was expecting a bashing, but no, she was calm about it. "We need to pray and may God's will be done," she said. "If God wants us to leave the UK to go to live in America, who am I to say no?" she concluded.

After completing the application package, Dr. Bullock called to arrange my flight to interview for the job. This was early April 2008. Looking through the aircraft window, I was terrified when I saw the runway at the Yeager Airport in Charleston, West Virginia. The airport is located on a small plain within the heavily forested mid-Appalachian Mountains. Why the Yeager was built within mountain slopes and how pilots continuously successfully navigate aircrafts there is still a great wonder to me. Sarah Barton welcomed me at the arrival hall and drove me nearly seventy-seven miles to Parkersburg, north of Charleston. She checked me into the plush Blennerhassett Hotel. I was fatigued, and the long drive made it super exhausting. The northbound I-77 highway was in superb condition but extremely winding with numerous bends. Sarah was the project manager of the OVU Title III Project, which provided initial funding for the chemistry professor position. She handed me a pack of hotel meal coupons and a detailed interview itinerary. She promised that Dr. Hardy would pick me up at 8:00 a.m. the following morning at OVU. I was starving but felt too tired to find dinner. I had a hot shower, prayed with Evelyn on the phone, and went straight to bed.

Dr. Hardy picked me up the following morning and showed me around the OVU campus. I was quite disappointed. The college was so tiny. The facilities seemed so old and poor. That reminded me about my first visit to the Asafo Church of Christ in Ghana. The church was so small and looked wretched. Immediately, I recalled Brother Stephen's scriptural advice years ago: "God does not dwell in temples made by human hands." God uses poor humble things to achieve great glory. The story of the virgin birth quickly struck me, and that kept me calm. Academic interviews can be quite long and exhaustive. After lunch, I taught a General Chemistry II class on nuclear chemistry. The interview panel included students, science professors, the dean of arts and sciences, and the provost. The interviews went well. I retired to my hotel before sunset. Evelyn was curious about the interview outcome. It was late in England, but she still stayed up to talk and pray with me. The following day's interviews were more relaxed. I had separate meetings with the dean, provost, chief finance officer, OVU president, and the board chairman.

The rest of the day was earmarked for touring the ancient cities of Parkersburg and Marietta and their Wood and Washington Counties. At the mention of Washington County, I asked if we could also visit Washington, DC. "No way," said Dr. Hardy, with a broad smile. "Washington, DC, is about six hours drive from here," he said.

"What?" I exclaimed. "I thought Virginia is very close to Washington, DC," I said.

"Yes, Virginia is close to DC, but we are not in Virginia. We are actually in West Virginia. In fact, Virginia is still about six hours drive away from Parkersburg," said Hardy. "West Virginia is a completely different state from Virginia," he added. "But you are not alone. Many US citizens also get confused about Virginia and West Virginia," he explained. "You and your family will get the chance to visit DC many times when you finally move here," he concluded.

That was the first hint I was probably going to get the job. Still, I was disappointed that Parkersburg was nowhere near Washington, DC. I had given that false impression to my family back home in England already.

I shared my stories when I arrived back in England. Evelyn was quite excited. She believed God was behind our relocation to the US. But not our girls. They were quite unsettled. Understandably, they were anxious about leaving their friends behind and going to restart new schools in a completely unknown rural community. I counseled them, prayed with them, and told them biblical travel stories to give them hope. Immanuel was just too young to understand what was going on. A couple of days later, Dr. Bullock called to congratulate me on the job offer. Shortly, I received a package in the mail confirming the same. The package also contained other important documents including immigration papers, contract agreements, remuneration, pension, health benefits, flight tickets, and shipment. Time seemed like it was flying after that point. The US embassy in London advised us to travel to Ghana to benefit from an expedited visa process. Appointments at the London consulate were far too congested. That threw a wrench in our travel plans. I was under serious pressure for time. It was early July. My contract with OVU was supposed to start on August 1. We disposed of many of our personal belongings on the cheap and traveled to Ghana in the middle of July. Fortunately, our US visas were ready three days after our arrival in Ghana. Still, we were exhausted and weary.

When Africans live in the diaspora for a long time, they lose natural immunity to endemic tropical diseases like malaria. We began to feel sick after one week in Accra. My body felt like coming down with malaria, but I had too little time to see a physician. I saw my pharmacist friend, Nelson, who administered malaria drugs. I felt better a day or two later. The next day, we traveled on board a KLM flight via Amsterdam to Detroit. Less than two hours before landing at the Amsterdam Schiphol Airport, I suffered some health scare. Going to use the backside aircraft lavatory, I felt very dizzy suddenly, fainted, and badly hit the aisle. Mercifully, I regained consciousness quickly. All I heard was Evelyn screaming, "Please help, please help, my husband is dying, please help." I was shivering terribly. The crew were very professional. They calmed my family down. Then they reclined me at the back seat, measured my vital signs, administered oral rehydration, covered me with blankets, and gave Tylenol to help reduce my fever. When we finally landed, an ambulance took me to the Schiphol airport clinic, where my blood samples revealed malaria parasites. They provided emergency treatment and relayed messages to Detroit Airport and OVU to continue my treatment upon arrival in West Virginia. In the subsequent weeks, Drs. Hopkins and Bagee (an Ethiopian physician) provided further care for Immanuel and me at the Camden-Clark Memorial Hospital until we were fully treated for malaria.

In the late afternoon on August 6, we were met on arrival at the Charleston Yeager Airport by a team of OVU faculty and staff. There were about four or five Americans. They were generous and professional. They drove us to our university residence at Parkersburg. Large trays of pizza were set up for dinner. After off-loading our luggage, our hosts departed. Our four-bedroom accommodation located near the Blennerhassett Island on the banks of the Ohio River was new, plush, and well furnished. The area was beautiful but quiet with only a few neighbors. Our things were scattered everywhere. We were too tired and sick to bother about which luggage contained what. Just before sunset, our doorbell rang. We were scared to answer the door.

"Who must be at the door?" Evelyn asked.

"We just arrived in this country, and nobody knows us," I added. "Our OVU hosts have all left, so who must be this?" I questioned. "We don't even have a phone to call the police if there is danger," I said.

"Don't open the door, Steve," Evelyn said. The door rang the second, then the third time.

"I will have to find out who the person is and face the situation one way or the other," I said. I asked Evelyn and our kids to move to the upstairs bedroom and lock themselves in. "Lock yourself up and be safe in case I get hurt," I said. I went to the door.

"Hello, my name is Debbie, and I am your next-door neighbor," she said. "I was told you and your family would be arriving from Great Britain today, and you're the OVU's new chemistry professor, correct? I came to greet you and family, introduce myself, and bring you food. You must be very tired and hungry," she said. Debbie handed me a big basket of fruits, bottled water, delicious-smelling covered casserole, and cheesecake dessert.

"Please come in." I beckoned Debbie. She came in. I called Evelyn and the kids from upstairs.

"This is Debbie, our next-door neighbor," I said. "She came in to greet us and to bring us food," I added. Debbie talked with us for nearly thirty minutes before departing. She became our friend and close contact ever since.

Our first experience with American culture was a very positive one. We were initially scared to answer the door because of Debbie. Where we previously lived in Great Britain, people were generally nice and possessed a great sense of humor, but like other Europeans, it was hard for them to warm to visitors they did not know personally. The experience with Debbie was opposite. Evelyn and I assumed danger rather than acquaintanceship and did what we could to protect our family. Whether Debbie's gesture was an everyday American culture is difficult to tell, but the fact remains that the life of people with strong religious beliefs always showed in their hospitality to strangers (Hebrews 13:2; Romans 12:13; 1 Peter 4:9).

During the first two weeks in August 2008, Dr. Kurt Huhtanen, my predecessor, generously spent time showing me around the science department, laboratories, classrooms, and offices. We also went through the science curriculums, books and published materials, hard and software resources, and he provided me with detailed handover notes. Was that good for me? Most certainly. I was a little bit too tired to understand all the things he wanted to show and tell me. Although Kurt had some wonderful materials I could use, my main responsibility was to create a new chemistry program with matching new curriculums. I had to first figure out how I was going to set up my four general chemistry and related courses for the fall semester. I was used to teaching one or two courses per semester in England, not four. This clearly was unfamiliar territory—new department, new colleagues, culturally new category of students, teaching resources, course management system, instructional technology. In fact, new everything! That seemed daunting a task. "Am I up to this onerous responsibility?" I asked myself. "God is my helper," I said in a consoling tone.

Before the start of fall classes, I was working in my office one quiet Saturday morning when someone knocked at my door. I had not seen anyone in the department all morning. When I opened the door, a staggering man about fifty years old asked whether he could come in. That scared me in a moment. I welcomed him and gave him a seat.

"My name is Larry Ice, the OVU Bookstore manager," he said.

"My name is Steve Opoku-Duah, the new associate professor of chemistry," I replied.

"You and your family are from Great Britain, is that correct?" Larry asked.

"Well, we moved here from Great Britain, but we are not British," I replied.

"So where are you guys from?" he asked.

"We are from Ghana, a small country in the western part of Africa," I responded.

"Oh, okay. What made you choose to come to OVU?" Larry asked further.

A rather long conversation ensued.

Larry liked to talk. He was a very smart man with a great sense of humor. Before leaving my office, he threw me an invitation to become his friend. Additionally, he requested my family to consider becoming members of the Grand Central Church of Christ where he served as a deacon and his son served as the youth minister. Graciously, I accepted his friendship request but asked for time to pray through church membership with my family. Larry told me about his health problems and requested me to pray with him. He discussed his struggles with Parkinson's disease and explained why he staggered while walking. We prayed about all that before he left.

Not a single day passed without Larry stopping by my office for a brief chat after we first met. All the time, he would remind me to visit the Grand Central Church of Christ. Larry was so nice, and our friendship grew rapidly. After visiting Grand Central a few times, we decided to place membership there. Larry was greatly pleased when Joe Spivy, the pulpit minister, publicly announced our decision to place membership with the congregation. Larry invited Evelyn and me to join their "Small Group." The "Small Group Ministry" is arguably one of the best organizational programs of the Grand Central Church. Its central goal is relational, designed to foster edification, spiritual and emotional support, group Bible study, meal fellowship, benevolent projects, and evangelism. A little boy called Jake Herridge wrote my son, Immanuel, a letter welcoming him to be part of the children's church. Grand Central (GC) is 99 percent Caucasians, but we probably would never experience any better brotherly love in this country than we ever had there. A few weeks later, the women's group treated us to a lavish shower, filling our house with gifts. Because of that generosity, we never purchased new home decor, crockery, chinaware, and cutlery for ten years. Details of other Grand Central stories are deferred later.

The OVU has one of the most rigorous academic programs in the US. The best part is dedicated faculty and staff, complemented by a strong liberal arts program, small classes, and spiritual mentorship instructed in a serene hilly and woody campus. As expected, the first couple of years was some of my most challenging times as a chemistry professor. This was not because of professional or pedagogical bankruptcy but mainly because of cultural disconnect. My English accent was and has been a big problem for many of my students. Like many Africans, English is my second language. I started learning English before age six. Over time, however, I have developed a complex mix of African and British accents. Many of my students found it confusing and hard to understand my instructions in the classroom and the laboratory. Studying the hard sciences like chemistry is a tough call. It gets murkier when students can hardly follow the instructor. Many freshmen, especially, openly criticized my accent and instructions. The same accent which was previously considered posh among my African and British students was now strange, weird, and incomprehensible in America. One day, one of my students ranted angrily about my instruction to the margins of disrespect. Her behavior greatly irritated me. I went home frustrated. Like always, Evelyn was there to console me. She advised me to be patient and gentle on the job. She requested for a copy of my class schedule and consistently prayed for me five minutes before each class for nearly two years. The results were amazing. What my students failed to recognize, however, was that I also struggled numerous times to understand their regional American accent. Cultural disconnect was to blame. A couple more examples specific to this matter are recounted in the subsequent section.

While discussing the physics behind seismic measurement of earthquakes in my physical geology class one day, I referred to an experience of earth tremors in my "outhouse apartment" several years ago in Ghana. The students burst into uncontrolled laughter. I was surprised. "This is nothing funny," I said.

One student replied, "Sir, that sounds very funny because we cannot imagine how you ever lived in a toilet." That was the first time I recognized that in the country districts of America, an "outhouse" refers to a toilet. In another case, I requested my lab assistant to replace naphthalene with camphor for one of my organic chemistry labs. When I returned, the class was still not ready because the students could not find naphthalene or camphor in their materials tray. I was furious why the students had idled for more than thirty minutes without getting any work done. Later, one student, Mitch, called his physician father who explained that camphor was "moth balls." While it is called camphor in Great Britain, it is moth balls in the US. These examples helped me to devise several strategies to mitigate episodes of miscommunication. I decided to pre-teach Mitch before most of my difficult lectures. When the students found the comprehension of science concepts difficult, I used Mitch to explain to the class, which perfectly worked as a peer-to-peer instructional approach.

One of the requirements of the OVU Title III Project was for me to develop a new chemistry program. I used the first year to do feasibility studies of the project. As a first step, I reviewed reports previously produced by Dr. Huhtanen and Mr. Gordon Wells. Next, I inventoried laboratory space, equipment, chemicals and reagents, technology, and other instructional resources. Our faculty needs, laboratory space, and chemistry accreditation requirements were also reviewed. The studies revealed the college's unreadiness for mounting a full chemistry degree program. Fortunately, resources were adequate for the creation of a biochemistry degree program in the 2010 academic year. Curricula for upper-level courses including Advanced Organic Chemistry, Inorganic Chemistry, Analytical Chemistry, and Biochemistry were created. Along with existing lower-level courses, the new program was matched against program requirements by the American Chemical Society. The program was then compared with similar faith-based universities in the US and small public universities in West Virginia. The dean's council and the academic board later reviewed the curriculum. The document was further updated and later approved by the university governing board. In addition, I created two new lab-based general education courses—physical geology and twenty-first-century science. The latter was a broad-based science course designed to instruct contemporary science topics including climate change, green energy, stem-cell research, biotechnology, forensic science, and nanoscience. The above program has helped to graduate hundreds of biology and biochemistry science majors across the country, many of whom are now working as physicians, dentists, pharmacists, nurses, engineers, and teachers.

In December 2012, OVU's executive vice president, Jeff Dimick, introduced me to his two friends, Messrs. Mark Wiley and Dennis Johnson (both engineers), who expressed interest in a research collaboration to develop innovative water purification technologies for humanitarian and commercial purposes. Our partnership resulted in the development of the so-called *katharos* technology. *Katharos* is a Greek word, which means "clean" or "spiritual." The project was exciting, so I jumped at the opportunity. For more than six years, we codeveloped, tested, and evaluated water purification prototypes, starting from batch-treatment systems (e.g., "Trashcan" and "Waltzing Matilda") to the industrial ("Trailer Unit" and "MORIF") systems. The humanitarian prototype consisted of an electrocoagulation unit built with a four-hundred-gallon steel tank powered by a high-amperage and low-voltage generator designed to provide energy via a five-second switching polarity from direct current electric discharge. The system was characterized by thirty-four-paired submerged anode and cathode cross-linked aluminum electrodes secured over the steel tank. The cross-linked electrodes produced the reverse polarity. The coagulator worked by establishing an intense electromagnetic field creating simultaneous oxidation-reduction reactions. A high-pressure pump was attached which channeled polluted water over the metal plate contact areas and ran at thirty minutes intervals. The treated water was pumped into clean glass tanks and tested for purity. Three research articles were published in refereed chemistry and water treatment journals while several reports were produced to document the industrial application of the Katharos technology.

After more than ten years at OVU, it was time to explore new academic opportunities. Was this decision easy? Not at all! I was quite well settled in West Virginia. I had made very good friends there. Indeed, I had made Parkersburg my home. Still, three important reasons motivated my exit. First, my academic job ran under serious threat. The OVU seriously struggled with financial problems. There is no gainsaying that higher education funding is now a serious global problem. Like many countries, two broad categories of higher education institutions are recognized in the US—public and private universities and colleges. OVU is a predominantly four-year baccalaureate small private college. In addition, it is a faith-based nonprofit institution that largely depends on student tuition fees and donor support to operate successfully. Unfortunately, funding sources have dwindled over the past two decades because of low student enrollment and depressed donor support. Several reasons have accounted for OVU's low student enrollment. Their overaged physical infrastructure and outdated academic facilities do not attract students. Nonetheless, tuition fees have risen nearly 10–15 percent in the past ten years. Meanwhile, tuition in comparable public institutions in West Virginia has improved because of the strong push for college education to be free countrywide. This relentless political agenda has the potential to eliminate competition for students in private faith-based universities and colleges in the country. Notice also that American students of today are more attracted to universities and colleges where they can find entertainment, active social life, and sports than colleges where social behavior is restricted and discipline is enforced because of faith goals. Students generally consider colleges in larger cities more fun than rural areas. Another reason why OVU's donor support has dwindled is the fact that their primary church constituency (Churches of Christ) has significantly declined in membership over the past three decades or so. While the older donor population are expiring, their replacement by a benevolent younger generation has not been entirely feasible.

When OVU started cutting staff and faculty jobs in 2017, I knew it was a good time to look for a new job. The problem was amplified by my "empty nest." My three children were college age and left home. I struggled with widowerhood and loneliness. I prayed to God to help me find a new job in a bigger city where I could experience a new way of life. I applied for several academic jobs, research, and industry. Between 2018 and 2019, I interviewed for three separate jobs in New York, Virginia, and California, but none of them produced a good fit. I specifically prayed to secure a new job before my summer mission trip to Ghana. By May 2019, I had not received any job interviews. One Friday evening, I saw a Lipscomb University advertisement for a chemistry professor in the *Christian Chronicle* newspaper. The application deadline was midnight the next day. It was impossible to complete the detailed online application before the deadline, so I sent my résumé directly to Dr. Kent Clinger, Lipscomb University's chair of chemistry to seek an extension to complete the application. Kent responded after church on Sunday afternoon. He asked me to provide unofficial transcripts, academic referees, and other relevant paperwork by Monday morning. That was a great relief. After one week, Ellie, the chemistry administrative assistant, called to arrange travel for me to interview for the job. Customary with academic jobs, the interview process was exhausting. It went well. I taught a class in general chemistry and gave a presentation on water purification using electrocoagulation. About a week later, I received congratulatory messages from Kent and the acting dean of the College of Liberal Arts and Sciences, Dr. Randy Bouldin, about their job offer.

"Praise God! Another miracle has occurred," I exclaimed.

I was faced with the challenge of whether to pursue the mission trip or cancel it. If I proceeded, I was going to be limited by time. If I canceled, students who had signed up would be greatly disappointed having spent nearly one year preparing for the trip. Satan never ceases to cast doubts in the mind of believers. While still raging in debate, the biblical story of the four lepers and the lifting of the great siege on Israel came to mind. I meditated upon 2 Kings 7:3–20. Shortly, the siege on my mind was lifted. Although there were challenges, including a serious illness, the mission trip proceeded successfully. We arrived back in the US in time to commence my new job in early August.

Now there were four men with leprosy at the entrance of the city gate. They said to each other, "Why stay here until we die? If we say, 'We'll go into the city'—the famine is there, and we will die. And if we stay here, we will die. So, let's go over to the camp of the Arameans and surrender. If they spare us, we live; if they kill us, then we die."

At dusk they got up and went to the camp of the Arameans. When they reached the edge of the camp, no one was there, for the Lord had caused the Arameans to hear the sound of chariots and horses and a great army, so that they said to one another, "Look, the king of Israel has hired the Hittite and Egyptian kings to attack us!" So they got up and fled in the dusk and abandoned their tents and their horses and donkeys. They left the camp as it was and ran for their lives.

The men who had leprosy reached the edge of the camp, entered one of the tents and ate and drank. Then they took silver, gold and clothes, and went off and hid them. They returned and entered another tent and took some things from it and hid them also.

Then they said to each other, "What we're doing is not right. This is a day of good news and we are keeping it to ourselves. If we wait until daylight, punishment will overtake us. Let's go at once and report this to the royal palace."

So they went and called out to the city gatekeepers and told them, "We went into the Aramean camp and no one was there—not a sound of anyone—only tethered horses and donkeys, and the tents left just as they were." [11] The gatekeepers shouted the news, and it was reported within the palace.

The king got up in the night and said to his officers, "I will tell you what the Arameans have done to us. They know we are starving; so, they have left the camp to hide in the countryside, thinking, 'They will surely come out, and then we will take them alive and get into the city.'"

One of his officers answered, "Have some men take five of the horses that are left in the city. Their plight will be like that of all the Israelites left here—yes, they will only be like all these Israelites who are doomed. So, let us send them to find out what happened."

So they selected two chariots with their horses, and the king sent them after the Aramean army. He commanded the drivers, "Go and find out what has happened." They followed them as far as the Jordan, and they found the whole road strewn with the clothing and equipment the Arameans had thrown away in their headlong flight. So, the messengers returned and reported to the king. Then the people went out and plundered the camp of the Arameans. So, a seah of the finest flour sold for a shekel, and two seahs of barley sold for a shekel, as the LORD had said.

Now the king had put the officer on whose arm he leaned in charge of the gate, and the people trampled him in the gateway, and he died, just as the man of God had foretold when the king came down to his house. It happened as the man of God had said to the king: "About this time tomorrow, a seah of the finest flour will sell for a shekel and two seahs of barley for a shekel at the gate of Samaria."

The officer had said to the man of God, "Look, even if the LORD should open the floodgates of the heavens, could this happen?" The man of God had replied, "You will see it with your own eyes, but you will not eat any of it!" And that is exactly what happened to him, for the people trampled him in the gateway, and he died. (2 Kings 7:3–20)

While in Ghana, I suffered food poisoning. I experienced a bout of bloody diarrhea and stomach infection. I was admitted to the Okomfo Anokye Teaching Hospital in Kumasi for four days. Before we returned to the US, I had become severely anemic and dehydrated. I had only three days to start my new job. First, I needed to move houses from West Virginia to Tennessee. At Nashville, I checked in at the Vanderbilt University Medical Center for further treatment before starting work. The story of the four lepers is a great inspiration to me.

I commenced my new faculty position at Lipscomb University on August 10, 2019. David Lipscomb and James A. Harding founded the Lipscomb University in 1891. The campus consists predominantly of the former estate of David Lipscomb, who donated it to the university in the Green Hills district. Like OVU, Lipscomb is a Christian liberal arts university affiliated with the Churches of Christ. Its seminary college has trained several ministers and Christian leaders from all over the world. Aside from its main campus, Lipscomb maintains two satellite locations called Spark in the Cool Springs area of Franklin (Tennessee) and Downtown Nashville. These campuses are designed to serve the business community. The U.S. News & World Report ranks Lipscomb University eighteenth among regional universities (South) according to its *2015 America's Best Colleges* guidebook. Lipscomb's liberal arts curriculum includes a wide range of academic programs in the arts and sciences. The curriculum continues to evolve, notably with the addition of civil and environmental engineering in the Raymond B. Jones College of Engineering and doctorate in pharmacy in the College of Pharmacy and Health Sciences. Under the administration of President Randy Lowry, Lipscomb has increased its graduate programs from eight to nearly fifty over the past decade.

My teaching and faculty responsibilities at the chemistry department were not significantly different from my previous role at OVU. As expected, the first academic year was challenging. This was compounded by the COVID-19 global pandemic, which hit in the spring semester. Still, the year ended successfully. At the start of my second year, I was appointed chair of the department. The role combined teaching and leadership functions. The details about my settlement in Nashville, Lipscomb, and the Brentwood Church of Christ are described in the subsequent chapter. The chapter further discusses my battle with anxiety and the effects of COVID-19.

9

Reverse Missions

I love mission work. I love believers who take mission work seriously. I owe my passion to Brother Stephen, my mentor and father in the Lord. The true purpose of missions is Jesus the Lord himself. Jesus came down on earth with one purpose: to search and to save. In other words, he came down to give eternal life to those who are lost and who believe (John 10:7–10).

> Then Jesus said to them again, "Most assuredly, I say to you, I am the door of the sheep. All who ever came before Me are thieves and robbers, but the sheep did not hear them. I am the door. If anyone enters by Me, he will be saved, and will go in and out and find pasture. The thief does not come except to steal, and to kill, and to destroy. I have come that they may have life, and that they may have it more abundantly. (John 10:7–10)

While Jesus clearly demonstrated the purpose of his earthly ministry, he also exemplified the same through teaching examples and methods (Luke 10).

After these things the Lord appointed seventy others also and sent them two by two before His face into every city and place where He Himself was about to go. Then He said to them, "The harvest truly is great, but the laborers are few; therefore, pray the Lord of the harvest to send out laborers into His harvest. Go your way; behold, I send you out as lambs among wolves. Carry neither money bag, knapsack, nor sandals; and greet no one along the road. But whatever house you enter, first say, 'Peace to this house.' And if a son of peace is there, your peace will rest on it; if not, it will return to you. And remain in the same house, eating and drinking such things as they give, for the laborer is worthy of his wages. Do not go from house to house. Whatever city you enter, and they receive you, eat such things as are set before you. And heal the sick there, and say to them, 'The kingdom of God has come near to you.' But whatever city you enter, and they do not receive you, go out into its streets and say, 'The very dust of your city which clings to us we wipe off against you. Nevertheless, know this, that the kingdom of God has come near you.' But I say to you that it will be more tolerable in that Day for Sodom than for that city. (Luke 10:1–12)

Then comes his global charge for missions after his triumphant victory over death in Matthew 28.

And Jesus came and spoke to them, saying, "All authority has been given to Me in heaven and on earth. Go therefore and make disciples of all the nations, baptizing them in the name of the Father and of the Son and of the Holy Spirit, teaching them to observe all things that I have commanded you; and lo, I am with you always, even to the end of the age." (Matthew 28:18–20)

No biblical passages better describe the essence and approach to church mission than the above. I developed a knack for mission work in my early tween years. Since then, I have been involved in local, national, and international missions. As young adults, Evelyn and I created a team that planned and executed outreach to bring the gospel to all our friends in our local Asawasi neighborhood. For five years, we knocked at people's doors and studied the Bible with our friends. Through this effort, we turned the hearts of several young friends to God. A couple of them, like Prince, have already passed, but a number of them are strong believers serving and working for the Lord in our home country and abroad. This outreach project was beyond other numerous church campaigns we participated in the suburbs of Kumasi, including Asafo, Amakom, Asokwa, Bimpeh Hill, Roman Hill, Fanti New Town, and Adum. It is difficult to quantify the number of people we reached between 1981 and 1988. We may have reached out to hundreds and hundreds of people, many of whom we never knew.

Our mission efforts continued when we moved to Accra in 1989. Unfortunately, we were not as successful as Kumasi. Two reasons explain that. Settling in Accra was difficult. At the same time, we struggled to raise two infants. Still, we participated in several church campaigns in Accra and other places including Akuapem Mampong, Kpando Torkor, Enyan Denkyira, and Abetifi. Kpando Torkor is a little town on the Volta Lake. We traveled the patchy dusty winding road to Kpando and made a steep descent to Torkor. To safely access the Volta islands from Torkor, one must catch the only ferryboat. Without that, one must ride in one of the wobbly wooden canoes fitted with old smoky outboard motors. I remember one of the scariest mission trips to the Torkor-Volta islands among five missionaries in September 1999. The ferryboat had broken down when we got to the harbor. We debated whether to travel by canoe or abort the trip. Several cases of canoe accidents have been reported on Lake Volta because of its sheer size and turbulence. Volta is believed to be the largest artificial reservoir in the world based on the surface area. It is contained behind the Akosombo Dam (built in 1965) and generates a substantial amount of Ghana's electricity. It is completely within the country and has a surface area of about 8,502 square kilometers (3,283 square miles; 2,101,000 acres). It extends from Akosombo in the south to the northern part of the country. The lake is very turbulent during the tropical rainstorms in September. Unfortunately, there are huge submerged timber stumps in the deepest parts of the lake. These stumps can dangerously imperil lake travel. There are numerous media reports describing submerged timber damage to boat and canoe hulls, leading to serious accidents and loss of lives. The local canoes are not well maintained and driven by "slave boys," some of whom can be less than ten years old. We prayed, put on our life jackets, and went aboard a small canoe. Natives living on the small Volta islands are anglers and very poor. The islands have no schools, brick houses, roads, and social amenities. Their only means of transport is by canoes and rafters. For three days, we lived in tents in Dzokotokope, discussed the Bible in people's homes, and publicly discussed biblical movies during nighttime. We baptized about sixteen men and women and planted a church there. Later, we established a primary school, provided borehole water, and started a small clinic to deliver babies and treat simple illnesses. Today, two more churches have been planted on other islands. The church has grown numerically, and the school has developed up to nine grade levels.

Our return from the island was not without drama. Our hired canoe man failed to show up. It was getting late. The village chief succeeded in finding us another boat, but it was slightly smaller than the first one. We crowded into it and began the one-and-a-half-hour journey back to the Torkor harbor. Unfortunately, the boy driver was not as skillful as the previous one. Besides, his canoe motor was not as efficient and required refueling twice. We were caught in darkness. Hardly could we see anything. "How safe are we?" we began to question one another. We prayed for God's help. Immediately, the story of Jesus and his disciples on the stormy waters of the Sea of Galilee came to my mind. I retold the story to calm down the crew. Using our flashlights and with the belief that Jesus was with us in the canoe, we anchored safely.

Sometime in 1997, I participated in a weeklong mission trip to Yendi, in the northern region of Ghana. Yendi is the largest town and administrative capital of the municipality, with a population of nearly sixty thousand. It also serves as the seat of the Dagomba Kingdom, where Yaa Naa, the king of the Dagomba people, has his royal palace. This makes Yendi a very important cultural center. The people of Yendi are mainly peasant farmers who grow grains and pulses including corn, Guinea corn, millet, soybeans, and peanut. They also cultivate tuber crops like yam. Additionally, Yendi serves as a commercial hub because of its location in the middle of several towns and villages in the northern corridor. Most people traveling to Tamale and beyond from the Eastern corridor, for instance, must go through Yendi. This makes it an important transport hub. Majority of the population in Yendi are Muslims, including the king. Therefore, the necessity of preaching the gospel of Jesus Christ is present. That is why evangelists like Nsoah, Dan McVey, Adams, and Adotey took up the missionary challenge in the area in the early 1990s. With financial help from friendly churches in the US, the Churches of Christ in Ghana have established a School of Preaching, Clinic, and Church of Christ Water Development Project in Yendi.

I traveled on missions in the company of Nsoah, Adams, Adotey, and Fred Asare. During daytime, we carried out field reconnaissance surveys or drilled wells while we preached the gospel in villages in the evenings. We also taught classes at the preaching school. Because of my expertise in hydrology, I spend more time with the well-drilling crew scouting for clean potable water for distressed communities while teaching the Bible at the same time. Additionally, I helped to train community water and sanitation leaders to better manage environmental sanitation and borehole pump repairs. One Sunday morning, we went to church in one of the villages with a population of about two hundred. There, I greatly experienced God's immeasurable grace and the power of the gospel of Christ. Poverty was everywhere. Nearly thirty people trekked several miles very early in the morning in tattered clothes to hear the message of salvation preached.

The small church building was filled to capacity. Some of them were new converts while others were Muslims and pagans. We distributed clothing to those who came to church half-naked, including some elderly women. When I spoke to one of the attendees, this is what he said, "I am not ashamed of physical nudity. I am rather ashamed of spiritual nakedness. I am happy Jesus cares about the poor and can heal sick people like me," he added. By the time we left the village, nearly fifteen souls were saved—men, women, and children.

Previously, I mentioned mission efforts in Europe. More details follow. There is no gainsaying that Africa, Asia, and South America are currently experiencing explosive Christian growth and revival. On the contrary, Christianity has lost traction in Europe and the Western world over the past three to four decades. In a survey conducted by the Pew Research Center in 2018 and 2019, 65 percent of American adults described themselves as Christians. This was found to be about 12 percent lower than responses ten years ago. Meanwhile, the religiously unaffiliated share of the population consisting of people who described their religious identity as atheist, agnostic, or "nothing in particular" was at 26 percent, representing a nearly 10 percent increase per the last survey in 2009. Figure 1 below displays detailed statistics of religious decline in the US. The level of decline in Europe is even worse. Reports by Lifeway Christian Resources (2020) show that twice as many Christians lived in Europe than in the rest of the world combined in 1900. Today, both Latin America and Africa have more. By 2050, the number of Christians in Asia is expected to supersede Europe. Currently, Christianity is barely growing in Europe (0.04 percent rate) and only slightly better in North America (0.56 percent). Oceania (0.89 percent) and Latin America (1.18 percent) have marginally better rates, but the faith appears to be rapidly growing in Asia (1.89 percent) and Africa (2.89 percent). Based on the above statistics, the need for "reverse missions" is real and urgent. Europeans and Americans sent missionaries all over the world in the last two centuries to spread the gospel and to plant the church of the living God. It is time for Asians and Africans to evangelize the Western world. I discovered this in the mid-1990s while a graduate student in the Netherlands.

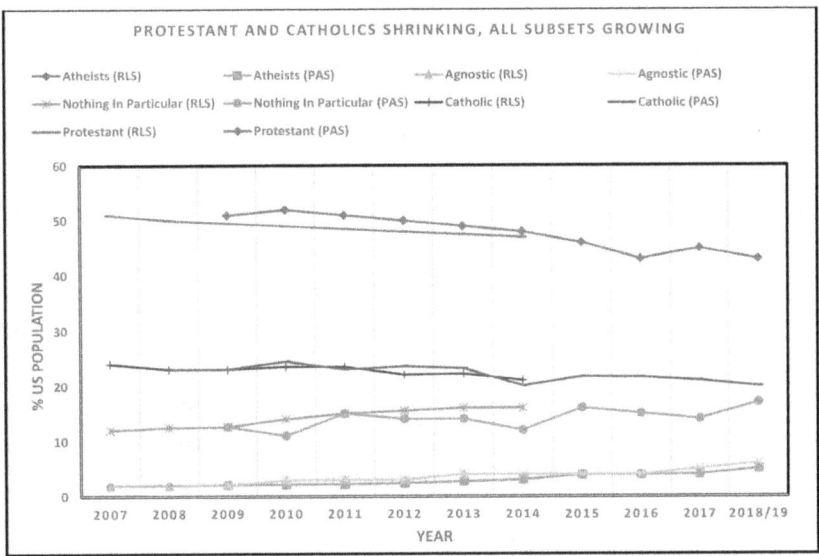

Figure 1. Religious affiliation in the US (Data reproduced following Pew Research Center, 2019)
Notes: (a) RLS = Pew Research Center Religious Landscape Studies (2007-2018); (b) PAS = Pew Research Center Political Surveys (2009-2019)

Religious affiliation in the US

In the Netherlands, Evelyn and I traveled many miles to go to church every Sunday. Meanwhile, other African immigrants struggled to find worship centers. We were motivated to plant a new church of Christ in Amsterdam. With the help of six Ghanaian friends, including Theresa and husband Donkor, we started the Amsterdam Church of Christ in 1995. In 1999, I returned to Amsterdam to work with the young church for nearly one year. Our immediate goal was to reach out to African immigrants and use those fluent in the Dutch language to reach out to the native Dutch people. We distributed gospel tracts at railway stations and discussed the Bible with people in public places. The response was positive. We purchased airtime and preached messages on the local Afro-Caribbean radio station. We invited listeners to ask biblical and social-cultural questions and answered prayer requests. We also held Bible studies in the Balmameer County at Kikkennstein. The patronage was encouraging. Today, there are two churches of Christ congregations in Amsterdam with the majority of them as immigrants. A couple of brethren who visited from Belgium and Germany planted new churches with the help of some American missionaries. Brother Ernest Boateng helped to nurture the African church in Hamburg and played a pioneering role in creating the now-vibrant European Bible lectureships. Every Easter, we brought in evangelists and Christian leaders from the US, Europe, and Africa to teach various biblical topics. In the Easter periods of 2018 and 2019, for example, I taught a series of Bible topics in Verona (Italy) and Milton Keynes (UK), respectively. Thirty-seven European immigrant churches participated in the Verona lectureships with a total attendance of 512. The cultural diversity of the European Bible lectureships keeps expanding every year. In 2019, for example, more than thirteen European congregations participated in the Milton Keynes program that discussed ways of fostering brotherliness and unity among the believers in the UK and Europe.

While working on a research project at the European Space Agency in Rome in 1998, I had a surprise call from one Ghanaian Christian worker in Italy called Regina, a resident of Vicenza. I knew Regina back home in Accra. Vicenza is one of the finest cities in northeastern Italy. She invited me to help with mission work in Vicenza. Her invitation immediately reminded me about Paul's vision in Troas concerning God's mission in the country of Macedonia—"Come over to Macedonia and help us" (Acts 16:9). Regina described a very exciting project. Their mission efforts had brought together nearly eighty immigrants together (believers and prospects) as part of the Church of Christ in Vicenza. The Vicenza church had previously been founded after World War II by American missionaries and was still overseen by American missionaries. An American missionary family was still working there when I first visited.

"We have problems in our church, and we will deeply appreciate it if you could come over and help us," Regina said.

"What problems?" I asked.

"The church has three culturally diverse groups—Americans, Italians, and Africans. Unfortunately, there is no harmony because of cultural differences and lack of spiritual maturity," she said. "Our American missionary and his family are preparing to return to the USA because of lack of sponsorship. The problem is that our Italian and African male brethren are not biblically knowledgeable and confident to lead the church when the minister leaves," she added. "Additionally, many of our African brethren continue to struggle with biblical doctrines regarding witchcrafts, reflection of the Law of Moses in today's church, and cultural integration. Could you please come over and teach some of these topics?" she asked.

"Absolutely!" I answered without thinking.

I discovered that Vincenza was nearly 350 miles away north of Rome. Air travel was quicker but quite expensive. Train or coach travel were possibilities. The Eurostar was about four hours train journey. The traditional night train was about six hours. Although night trains and coach travel are much cheaper, they can be quite boring and tiresome. As I considered my options, Satan suddenly began to sway my mind with several "what-if scenarios," seeking to dissuade me from God's work. Prior to that, I had heard several weird stories about robberies and hooligan attacks on sleeper trains. My mind began to wonder, *What if I faced an attack on the sleeper? What if I lost my way through the night? What if fatigue derailed my scientific research at the European Space Agency?* Fear began to grip me. I was tempted to abort my mission plans. Some voices began to emphasize the need for me to remain in Rome, focus on my research assignment, and remain safe. The Holy Spirit came to my rescue. *What if none of these things you are thinking about never happened? And what if you failed God's work and lost his blessings? And who says not traveling outside Rome is guaranteed safety?* My heart began to beat rapidly. My body began to feel warm. I decided to listen to the subtler voice. I stopped and prayed. I stabilized my thoughts. I rejected the notorious voice of Satan. "I will go to Vicenza every weekend to work with the Christians there no matter what," I said confidently.

One Friday night, I got on the night train from Roma Termini (central railway station), transited at Bologna, and arrived at Vicenza the following morning. The second-class train car was extremely noisy. I am not sure whether any of the passengers caught any sleep. We arrived safely. Two of the African brothers welcomed me on arrival at the Vicenza train station. Although that was our very first meeting, we still engaged in a hearty conversation on our way home as if we had known each other for many years. After a warm shower and breakfast, they took me to meet with Brother Jason, the American missionary. He spoke excitedly about his multiple years of mission work in Italy. He recounted the long history of the Vicenza church and rued the potential leadership vacuum upon his return to his home country. He welcomed my desire to help teach Bible classes and lead mission efforts in the area. Out of the over 120 church members, 70–80 percent of them were African immigrants. The rest were Italians, besides the American missionary family. Nearly 60 percent of the congregation were males. I met the African brethren at their weekend prayer meeting. Aside from Sister Regina, I knew two other couples from back home in Ghana. We developed a plan for Bible studies, leadership studies, and outreach. Already, some of them had Bible study prospects. They were clearly excited about my decision to be part of their mission efforts. I preached my first sermon on Sunday morning and taught the evening Bible class. I felt great satisfaction and inner peace as I reflected on my journey back to Rome. For nearly one year, I traveled to Vicenza every Friday night and returned to my research laboratory on Monday morning. As expected, the Rome-Vicenza journey back and forth was extremely stressful and exhausting. Still, I persevered.

After a few weeks, another mission opportunity presented. Two families who traveled nearly eighty miles to church from Verona spoke about their friends' interest to study how Jesus fulfilled the Law of Moses per his Sermon on the Mount in Matthew 5:17–18. Additionally, they wanted to understand the key differences between the Law of Moses and the Law of Christ (2 Cor. 3:1–6; 1 Cor. 9:21; Gal. 6:2). Apparently, their unchurched friends had been reading the Bible privately without proper understanding and needed help. I took up the challenge, and we started a new Bible discussion group.

> Do not think that I have come to abolish
> the Law or the Prophets; I have not come to
> abolish them but to fulfill them. For truly, I say
> to you, until heaven and earth pass away, not an

iota, not a dot, will pass from the Law until all is accomplished." (Matthew 5:17–18)

We traveled to Verona and spent several hours studying with the prospects. When they finally understood the fulfillment of the Old Testament prophecies about Jesus and primary differences between the Law of Moses and the Law of Christ (1 Cor. 9:21; Rom. 10:4, 6:14), they subjected themselves to baptism—there were five of them. For several weeks, they traveled from Verona to Vicenza to attend Sunday worship and midweek Bible studies. Shortly, they found the travels too tiring and time-consuming. We decided to plant a new church in Verona. The last time I visited Verona in 2019, the church had grown, with a membership of over two hundred people, with Brother Thomas, one of the African immigrants as their minister.

Through our pioneering missionary efforts in Amsterdam in the mid-1990s, many immigrant-based churches have now been planted across Europe. Today, there are more than forty immigrant Churches of Christ, majority of them in Great Britain. While living in England, Evelyn and I continued to work with and plant African churches. Immigrant churches continue to be planted in Western Europe, North America, Australia, Korea, Japan, and China. After nearly three decades, the impact of these immigrant churches on Western culture and church is beginning to show in a very important way. In 2008, for example, the membership of the Northland Church of Christ in Columbus (Ohio) was about 350. After ten years, Sunday church attendance had declined to less than 200. Today, there are three different worship services every Sunday: early morning American-English service, late-morning Spanish-speaking service, and after-noon African-speaking service. Brother Caleb Dillinger (American) is the senior minister. My family started working with the African church in 2009. At that time, their membership was less than fifty. Today, their membership has grown past 200. When their number overgrew their worship space, we planted a new church with Bro. Mike Alimo (from Ghana) as their minister. Interestingly, Both Mike and Caleb are alumni of the Bible Department of the Ohio Valley University. They are my former students too. Another example is the

Worcester Church of Christ. The majority of the nearly 150 members are African immigrants. Bro. Nat Kissi (from Ghana) currently serves as their pulpit minister. The Sampson brothers (from Ghana) also serve as evangelists for churches of Christ in the New York City District. Additionally, several other African immigrants continue to serve as church leaders (pastors, elders, deacons, evangelists, and mission leaders) across Europe and North America. In the last twenty years, African immigrants have planted more than twenty churches of Christ in the US and Canada. The Lord continues to bless these "reverse mission" efforts.

10

When Tragedy Strikes

Imagine a number of men in chains, all under sentence of death, some of whom are each day butchered in the sight of the others; those remaining see their own condition in that of their fellows and looking at each other with grief and despair await their turn. This is an image of the human condition.

—Blaise Pascal

Is the human condition full of trauma and despair? The answer depends on the responder. To the celebrant, the human condition is blissful. To the mourner, the human condition is full of misery. The truth is that the life of a mortal being is short yet full of trouble (Job 14:1–12) from the days of Adam. That is the reason why everyone needs God. Also, that is the reason why a poor mother's prayer is needed to change her son's destiny.

> Mortals, born of woman, are of few days and full of trouble. They spring up like flowers and wither away; like fleeting shadows, they do not endure. Do you fix your eye on them? Will you bring them before you for judgment? Who can bring what is pure from the impure? No one!

A person's days are determined; you have decreed the number of his months and have set limits he cannot exceed. So look away from him and let him alone, till he has put in his time like a hired laborer. At least, there is hope for a tree: If it is cut down, it will sprout again, and its new shoots will not fail. Its roots may grow old in the ground and its stum die in the soil, yet at the scent of water it will bud and put forth shoots like a plant. But a man dies and is laid low; he breathes his last and is no more. As the water of a lake dries up or a riverbed becomes parched and dry, so he lies down and does not rise; till the heavens are no more, people will not awake or be roused from their sleep. (Job 14:1–12)

Imagine that you lived more than three thousand miles away from home and trouble hit. Assume that you are in a foreign land without family, friends, and close acquaintances, and suddenly, disaster struck. In this case, the only person who you considered closest friend, mother, sister, spouse, and adviser suddenly left your world, and you have no hope of meeting her again. The loss is not only tragic; it is excessively heartbreaking! That is what happened on September 11, 2014, at 3:00 p.m.—Evelyn finally said goodbye to be with the Lord after a hard battle with cancer. That is the picture people like biblical Job and Blaise Pascal have painted as "image of the human condition." Will life ever transpire without trouble, grief, or despair? Certainly not. In the scriptures, James emphasizes that trials and temptations are inevitable in a believer's life (James 1:2–18). The excellent part is that successful "faith-testing" sufferers have the blessing of undergoing spiritual metamorphosis into overcomers to wear a "crown of life." Then comes along the development of enviable personal attributes including perseverance, maturity, completeness, wisdom, trust, steadfastness, humility, and boldness.

Consider it pure joy, my brothers and sisters, whenever you face trials of many kinds, because you know that the testing of your faith produces perseverance. Let perseverance finish its work so that you may be mature and complete, not lacking anything. If any of you lacks wisdom, you should ask God, who gives generously to all without finding fault, and it will be given to you. But when you ask, you must believe and not doubt, because the one who doubts is like a wave of the sea, blown and tossed by the wind. That person should not expect to receive anything from the Lord. Such a person is double-minded and unstable in all they do.

Believers in humble circumstances ought to take pride in their high position. But the rich should take pride in their humiliation—since they will pass away like a wildflower. For the sun rises with scorching heat and withers the plant; its blossom falls, and its beauty is destroyed. In the same way, the rich will fade away even while they go about their business.

Blessed is the one who perseveres under trial because, having stood the test, that person will receive the crown of life that the Lord has promised to those who love him.

When tempted, no one should say, "God is tempting me." For God cannot be tempted by evil, nor does he tempt anyone; but each person is tempted when they are dragged away by their own evil desire and enticed. Then, after desire has conceived, it gives birth to sin; and sin, when it is full-grown, gives birth to death.

Don't be deceived, my dear brothers and sisters. Every good and perfect gift is from above, coming down from the Father of the heavenly

lights, who does not change like shifting shad-
ows. He chose to give us birth through the word
of truth, that we might be a kind of first fruits of
all he created. (James 1:2–18)

Training is profitable for every human enterprise. Church missions are no exception. Since mid-1995, Evelyn and I have been
involved in international missions and training of young people,
including our own children. Our maiden activity in West Africa
happened in the summer of 2012. Six students from the Ohio
Valley University (West Virginia) and two chaperones joined the
team focused on rural missions. In partnership with the Sixth &
Washington Sts. (Marietta, Ohio) and Kojokrom Church of Christ
(Western Region, Ghana), we reached out to more than twenty villages, baptized thirty-six souls, and planted two churches. The high-
light was the conversion of a witch doctor and her entire family.
Witch doctors and voodoo practitioners command respect in rural
Africa because they are believed to possess powerful deities that are
capable of solving many everyday problems, including the treatment
of supposedly "spiritual illnesses." To many rural people, complex
illnesses like schizophrenia, infertility, sexual malfunction, and cancer bulk as "spiritual illnesses" only treatable by witch doctors. The
Mando village witch doctor was doubtlessly in this category. We visited their family home because her first son invited us. After two days
of Bible studies, the witch doctor abandoned her idols and deities
and converted to Christ. Like the Philippian jailer (Acts 16:16–34),
the woman and her four adult children were baptized into Christ.

Prior to our mission trip, Evelyn complained about a one-off
sharp pain in her breast. She suspected a small lump and decided to
see her doctor after our return to the US. According to her physician,
her mammogram results showed no disease. She reported again when
the pain persisted. When her physician insisted there was no reason
to be worried, we decided to see a specialist for a second opinion at
the Ohio State University Medical Center in Columbus, Ohio. It
was there we found out that Evelyn was suffering from the deadly
stage 3 triple-negative breast cancer. This was devastating news! We

cried and prayed all the way back home. Our fervent hope was that Jehovah God was going to intervene and bring healing to Evelyn's body. We also prayed for God to find us the best oncologist, oncological surgeon, and radiologist to treat her disease. As we sang, prayed, and cried, we lost track of our acceleration and shot over the highway speed limit. Suddenly, the blue flashing lights of cops beamed on us as we approached the first exit to Athens, Ohio, on US Route 33 W. A young cop pulled us over. He saw our tears. He asked the reason for our depression. We grudgingly confessed our sorrow and pleaded for clemency. He expressed sympathy but still emphasized the necessity for him to do his job. He ticketed us for overspeeding. That was my first-ever traffic violation. Thinking about it today, it feels like the officer was a bit heartless and mean.

We were too scared to tell our children about Evelyn's diagnosis when we arrived home. We first thought about concealing the information from them. Our daughters were grown up. They had just completed college education and had become young adults, full of knowledge and zest. Even our fourteen-year-old son could easily understand our family crisis. We finally broke the news to all of them when our daughters pressed us to know their mother's diagnosis. They were scared and cried openly. I called everyone together for family prayers that night, and all cried through the prayer. Evelyn was not only worried about her diagnosis but was also worried about the cost of cancer treatment. Thankfully, we had generous health insurance from my employers. I referred to that to allay her fears. Naturally, I was more worried about her survival of cancer than the money to pay for the treatment. We went back to see the oncological team at the Stefanie Spielman Comprehensive Breast Cancer Center in Columbus, Ohio, managed partly by the Ohio State University Medical Center. Evelyn's treatment options were very narrow. She was scheduled to undergo chemotherapy, surgery, and radiotherapy. Recovery was going to be slow and painful. Over several weeks, we traveled back and forth to Columbus for treatment. We lodged in a hotel for most surgery days.

Caring for my sick wife, taking care of my home and son's soccer practices and games, and teaching college classes were some of the most difficult times of my life. Week after week, I got more drained and wearier. That began to show in my physical appearance and demeanor. Some of my neighbors and friends at church began to talk me into asking for help. It was clear I could not handle all these by myself. Don and Elaine Lowe, an elderly neighbor we have adopted as "parents," decided to help by taking care of my son's school pick-ups, soccer practices, and soccer games. The women's group at church decided to help with errands and relieve me of some of the chemotherapy treatment trips to Columbus. Although they were incredibly helpful, Evelyn was still uncomfortable about help from nonfamily members because of her incessant pains. After about three months of treatment, Evelyn's health was restored, and she was declared cancer-free. Our family and church friends celebrated her remission as if all the treasures of heaven were couriered to our home address.

Evelyn agreed to join me for groceries at Walmart one cool Saturday afternoon in September 2013. Less than two miles away from home, she screamed hysterically, asking me to stop the car because she was feeling some strange electrical shock across her body from head to toe. Before I could pull up, I saw her removing her clothes. I was terrified and quickly rushed her to a nearby McDonald's fast-food store. I pleaded for the manager to call for an ambulance, shouting repeatedly: "My wife is fainting. My wife is dying." Before the ambulance arrived, Evelyn had regained consciousness and was feeling completely well. She asked us to return home, but the paramedics and I insisted for her to be fully checked out at the hospital. The ER doctor at the Parkersburg Camden-Clark Memorial Hospital was a Nigerian and highly professional. He reviewed Evelyn's cancer history and run a series of diagnostic tests. After a couple of hours, he called me into his office and gave me yet another devastating news:

"I am so sorry, Mr. Steve, your wife's cancer has returned. And the bad news is that it has metastasized into her brain, causing her seizure this afternoon. Her brain scans have revealed a large tumor, for which reason I will be referring her to see neuro-oncologists at the Ohio State University James Cancer Center in Columbus for further diagnosis and treatment."

When Satan strikes, the blow can be insanely deadly. My hands and feet began to shake violently. I felt like fainting. "Where is she?" I asked.

"Don't worry, she is well and relaxed," said the doctor. "But she must definitely see an oncologist and neurosurgeon as soon as possible. My recommendation is for you to go to Columbus tomorrow morning," he concluded.

We apprised our children about the new setback, teared up profusely, and prayed all that night. Early the following morning, Evelyn and I drove to Columbus to see the brain specialists. They were very professional. They explained Evelyn's condition to us clearly and run a number of very complicated tests. After about one week, when the test results arrived, the initial suspicion of a brain tumor was confirmed; recurrent breast cancer was predicted as the cause of her brain metastasis.

In one of the meetings with the specialists, we were told Evelyn ought to have a brain surgery to remove the tumor, without which her condition could deteriorate quickly, and she could possibly die. Both Evelyn and I were petrified. The brain surgery was scheduled for November 4. She was admitted to the hospital the day prior to surgery for preoperative counseling and assessment. The surgery was complex and long. I completely lost appetite and could not eat for nearly three days. All I did was keep praying for my wife. One of the elders of our church, Jeff Harper, decided to spend time at the hospital with me, praying and assuring me it would be well with Evelyn. I nearly collapsed when I was called in to visit Evelyn after surgery in the ICU. Her head was heavily dressed in thick metal braces. I was scared she was not going to survive. But the surgeons confirmed the surgery was so successful that they had executed a "full section of the brain tumor." "Full section" referred to "complete" removal of the tumor using the so-called Gamma Knife technology. Evelyn's recovery was remarkably exceptional. The surgeons were incredibly amazed at how she quickly exceeded all recovery benchmarks. After three days in the hospital, Evelyn was discharged, and we slowly drove home. Several postoperative review appointments followed, with many good days.

Unexpectedly, in early 2014, the neurologists found that Evelyn's brain tumor had started growing back. The doctors were unhappy, and we were greatly depressed. This time, it was not a single tumor but serious metastasis from the frontal lobe and other parts of the brain. This news was probably more devastating than all we have had for nearly two years. We came back home completely drained, depressed, and helpless. Then one of our friends at church suggested a second opinion about the brain scans from the Cancer Centers of America's (CCA) specialist facility in Chicago. We traveled to Chicago in early July to see one of the world's most respected neuro-oncologists—a Jewish doctor. He was extremely kind and professional. After he has run several scans of Evelyn's central nervous system, he concluded that even though Evelyn had very little chance of survival, he would give his best shot with a new treatment technology based on gene therapy. Before Evelyn could start the new treatment, her condition deteriorated so badly that she was completely paralyzed. Her condition continued to worsen day after day. She was not only bedridden but she could also not eat or drink; tube feeding was the only option.

All this while, I had lost so much time at work. So I decided to leave my first daughter, Godlive, behind in Chicago while I traveled back to West Virginia to request more time off at work and prepare for the worst. The next day, Evelyn's doctors called me to speedily return to Chicago because my daughter was also very ill. Not fully aware of her mother's terminal condition, she eavesdropped on a discussion by Evelyn's physicians about recommending hospice care, knowing her days were numbered. Godlive passed out and was admitted to care upon the news. When I heard about Godlive's situation too, I felt like choking; I could hardly breathe. My knees felt wobbly, and I could hardly talk. "How could I lose my spouse and my daughter at the same time? O God Almighty, help me," I prayed. One of my American friends, Harry, drove me nine hours that night to Chicago. Godlive had fully recovered when we arrived there. A few days later, our primary care physician, Dr. Hopkins, drove Evelyn back to West Virginia in a borrowed recreational vehicle to an arranged hospice in Marietta, Ohio. Because the hospice was not convenient and comfortable enough, we moved Evelyn into home hospice care. My daughters, Evelyn's friends (the Addo, Burrows, Wharton, and Hopkins families), and I tenderly cared for her until her final departure.

Evelyn seemed comfortable. She was at peace with her Maker all through those extremely difficult days until Tuesday, September 9. When I saw that she gravely struggled for breath and laid exceedingly frail, I called the elders of our church to come over and pray for her. That day, my children and I thought that was probably going to be our last day with her alive. She bravely prevailed like she has always done. She was restless, and that made us extremely nervous. The prayers of the elders calmed her until Thursday, September 11. I went to pick up my son from school around three o'clock while Abbe, Godlive, and my close friend, Freeman, attended to Evelyn. Just before I arrived at Parkersburg High School, Freeman called my phone to come back home immediately. I knew she was gone. Evelyn has always been wise. She was determined to depart while I was not present. Probably she knew I could faint at seeing her go away. I asked Freeman, "Is she gone home?"

"Yes, my brother," he answered, sobbing. How could I tell my son this? Immediately, I called my preacher friend, Joe Spivy, and asked him to summon the church elders for prayers in my house. I took my son to meet with Joe, and we carefully trained his attention to the disaster at home. My daughters were very brave. My teenage son was even braver. When he saw his lifeless mother on her bed, he kissed her hand, said a brief prayer, and pronounced his words of farewell! At that point, my bowels felt like crushing. It felt like I had lost my mind. I was inconsolable! I remembered I needed to be strong for my children. I wiped my tears and prayed to God for help. A few hours later, Evelyn was carried away to the funeral home, and that was the last time she literally spent time with us.

For more than three weeks, I planned Evelyn's funeral alongside the Grand Central Church of Christ and her family across the US. Her two younger sisters from Allentown, Pennsylvania, and cousins from Chicago and their families all arrived for the funeral. More than two hundred Ghanaian brethren across North America, Europe, and

Ghana arrived in West Virginia to celebrate Evelyn's beautiful and highly impactful life. Her funeral was an interesting mix between Ghanaian and American culture. Without a doubt, my children and I will continue to miss a true mother, wife, friend, sister, counselor, and champion. Nevertheless, we are happy she is in a better place without sorrow or pain (Revelation 12:4).

> And God shall wipe away all tears from their eyes; and there shall be no more death, neither sorrow, nor crying, neither shall there be any more pain: for the former things are passed away." (Revelation 12:4 NKJV)

There is nothing painful and atrocious than widowerhood. "It is not good for a man to be alone," says the Bible. Evelyn's battle with cancer and loss inflicted a debilitating toll on me. A week or so before her funeral, I felt so sick that my sister-in-law checked me into the Marietta Hospital ER. I suffered a serious bout of heartache, anxiety, and depression. I was in the hospital for three days. My family and friends were quite worried. Thankfully, I quickly recovered. Still, I was prescribed anxiety medications, which lasted for several months. After some time, I experienced serious side effects, but the physician thought the symptoms were something else. He was insistent for me to continue taking the medications, which I flatly refused. Even after discarding the treatment, it took nearly one year before I completely recovered from the symptoms and withdrawal effects.

My adult children have been a great source of comfort through these difficult times. When lonely, I benefited greatly from their encouragement and company. As time went on, they were obligated to leave home for college, making me very lonely. Being alone all the time was difficult. I prayed to God to help me through widowerhood and loneliness. My utmost desire was to find a new life partner. This was not easy. There were several bottlenecks. As a student of the Bible, I knew perfectly well that I could marry whoever I wanted, yet "only in the Lord" (1 Corinthians 7:39). Besides, I could only marry a woman qualified by biblical standards (Matthew 19:3–13). Then there is the question of love, romance, culture, age, social bonding, and physical distance. For several years, I struggled to find the right partner, without success. Over time, I learned a good lesson—it was best to leave the search in the hands of God. Still, loneliness is like darkness—it never disappears until light appears!

11

Bottled in by COVID-19

The term COVID-19, coined by the World Health Organization, refers to the coronavirus infectious disease of 2019. The actual medical term for the disease is SARS-CoV-2, which means severe acute respiratory syndrome coronavirus-2. *Corona* is the Greek word for crown, from which coronaviruses obtain their name because of their similar molecular shape.

Coronaviruses are a large family of viruses that usually cause mild to moderate upper respiratory tract illnesses, including common cold (NIH—National Institute of Allergies and Infectious Diseases, 2012). Over the past two decades, however, three new coronaviruses have emerged from animal reservoirs, causing serious and widespread illnesses and death to humans. There are hundreds of coronaviruses, most of which circulate among animals like pigs, camels, bats, and cats. Sometimes those viruses jump to humans, which scientists refer to as the "spillover event." This is the main source of diseases to humans. Four of the seven known coronaviruses that sicken people cause only mild to moderate disease. The remaining three can cause more serious, even fatal, disease including severe acute respiratory syndrome (SARS coronavirus or SARS-CoV-2). SARS-CoV-2 was detected in November 2002. Thankfully, the virus disappeared by 2004. Then in September 2012, the Middle East Respiratory Syndrome (MERS-CoV) emerged. Scientists determined that the virus transmitted from an animal reservoir in camels to humans and continues to cause sporadic and localized outbreaks. The third novel coronavirus to emerge in this century is the so-called SARS-CoV-2, believed to have emerged from China in December 2019 (COVID-19) and declared a global pandemic by the World Health Organization (WHO) on March 11, 2020. The effects of COVID-19 on the global population and economy have been incalculable. We know that COVID-19 emerged from China. But how was it transmitted to humans? Did it emerge naturally, or it was deliberately engineered to wreak havoc to benefit a section of human society? This is a question whose answer has probably been tossed by conspiracy theorists than scientists or rational thinkers. Many scientists, media personnel, and political commentators have postulated that the actual source of COVID-19 may never be found. I differ from this position. One day, the correct source may be found. My belief is that the valid source may be ascertained when the information is no longer needed.

As a scientist, I will be the last person to dwell on conspiracy theories instead of pursuing rational and valid solutions to human and environmental problems. I know that nature and human interference can aid the emergence of viruses. This has happened before. We know about century-old influenza, SARS, MERS, and the extremely annoying common cold coronaviruses. Unfortunately, these examples have done little to quell the contradictory and sometimes ridiculous theories about the source of COVID-19. Some people have assumed a laboratory accident or intentionally engineered a conspiracy aimed at Bill Gates and his empire's prosperity. Others have talked about the global political authority pursuit by the Chinese Communist Party and the 5G wireless network infrastructure designed to usher in the new world order. The Wuhan virus research lab has been accused of conducting "gain-of-function" research, which may have culminated in viral disease proliferation, including COVID-19. When virologists talk about "gain-of-function" research, they are referring to research projects that alter viruses in a way that can make them more transmissible and can allow viruses to hop to new hosts, like human beings, very easily. Unfortunately, the credibility of these theories is hard to ascertain. Most recently, however, there have been intelligence reports revealing how Wuhan Institute of Virology (WIV) researchers fell sick with symptoms like COVID-19 long before the Chinese government announced the emergence of the disease. The US intelligence reports have further disclosed that many WIV scientists were hospitalized in November 2019, fueling the suspicion of a cover-up. In May 2021, for instance, Dr. Robert Redfield, a former director of the US Centers for Disease Control and Prevention speculated that the virus most likely leaked from Wuhan laboratory by accident. The World Health Organization (WHO) and Dr. Anthony Fauci flatly refuted Redfield's allegations. These reports triggered a call by US President Joe Biden for his intelligence agencies to unravel the real source of COVID-19 by the end of August 2021. What may have happened based on scientific research and WHO analysis is that the coronavirus may have jumped from animal species to humans and mutated with rapid transmissibility compared to previous pandemics like the SARS and MERS. My prediction is that a wild animal slaughtered for food (e.g., cave nectar bat) may have carried the infectious virus to humans in either Wuhan lab or its fish market. It is not impossible that some scientists may have carried the virus to the laboratory from home or vice versa. In addition, one must remember that long viral incubation and viral loads cannot be ignored when discussing disease transmissibility, infection rate, time, space, human hosts, and travel.

The US and other foreign media started talking about COVID-19 in early February 2020. We now know that the disease was probably present globally several months before China and the WHO announced its presence. In March 2020, then—US President Donald Trump announced measures to curb its spread in the US, including travel bans to China, Europe, and many parts of the world. On March 11, 2020, the WHO declared COVID-19 as a global pandemic, making it the first of such designation since the declaration of H1N1 influenza or swine flu in 2009. Like many US citizens, President Trump and some of his senior officials assumed the disease was going to go away like a fleeting hurricane without trouble. That was not the case. By the end of the year, there were more than 23 million confirmed coronavirus cases and at least 500,000 deaths according to data published by the US Center for Disease and Prevention Control (CDC) and Johns Hopkins Medical Center COVID-19 Tracking Center. Globally, the WHO reported more than 182 million confirmed COVID-19 cases in July 2021, with over 3.9 million deaths, these numbers undoubtedly underestimate the real toll. Thankfully, by June 2021, more than 140 million Americans were reported to have been fully vaccinated, representing nearly 43 percent of the national population.

Following the COVID-19 detection, the CDC announced comprehensive protocols to help prevent the spread of the disease. In the main, citizens were requested to watch for symptoms until fourteen days after exposure. If people were found symptomatic, they were asked to immediately self-isolate and contact their local public health authority or healthcare provider. But whether infected or not, the US population was mandated to wear a face mask, stay at least six feet from others, wash their hands, avoid crowds, and take other steps to prevent the spread of the disease. Still, the damage of the disease was incalculable. The US was the most hit compared to all other nations. The reason for the devastation was more of a cultural and political problem than anything else. Americans are independent thinkers and simply abhor authoritative instructions. The editor of the Chinese state-owned *Global Times* newspaper, Hu Xijin, once tweeted after the US national elections that "President Trump and the first lady have paid the price for their gamble in playing down the impact of Covid-19." Many Americans still believe that President Trump lost the December 2020 general elections partly because of his unserious consideration of the dangers of the pandemic. His failure to recognize COVID-19 as a war against his nation and the world was considered a great miscalculation.

Aside from its debilitating illness and loss of lives, the extraneous effects of COVID-19 on humanity will remain immeasurable many decades hereafter. Despair, mental illness, job losses, economic recession, derailed human comfort, religious sanctuary shutdowns, school and college closures, and global depression will remain unforgettable. The fixing of the global economic recession may take several years. Without a doubt, poverty will be exacerbated in the developing world. Nevertheless, COVID-19 has taught our world very important lessons. First, global preparedness for pandemics must surely improve. The good part is that our modern society has now learned new ways to survive troubling times. New coping skills have now been developed by both old and young people. Who knew that many traditional jobs could still be done effectively from home instead of the workplace? Alternatively, who thought that homes could serve as classrooms or religious sanctuaries? What about the development and use of technology to meet the needs of business, teaching and learning, religious sanctuaries, and other social and economic activities?

Like many Americans, I do not know whether I ever suffered COVID-19 or not. On the two occasions when I experienced COVID-19 symptoms, I still tested negative. The fear of the disease was emotionally draining. Aside from the loss of my wife, never have I suffered loneliness, anxiety, fear, and emotional discomfort any year than 2020. I moved to Tennessee alone to take up a new academic position. I hardly knew my way around Nashville. I never knew anyone and had no friends. I was beginning to acquaint myself with my new academic environment and faculty colleagues. I had just found a church family but hardly knew anyone. When I was beginning to feel welcome, COVID-19 suddenly hit so hard. Lipscomb University, like other colleges, decided to close in the last week of March 2020. Everyone was scared to travel. I could not travel to visit my children. They could not travel to see me either. Something happened one day. My daughter's car broke down, and she flew down from Pennsylvania to pick up my second car. She was utterly shocked when I refused her attempt to hug me. She had not seen me for more than one year. She was brave and ready to hug, but I was scared to do so. I feared COVID-19 infection. I sanitized her completely before allowing her into my apartment. I remained shut-in for the most part of the year, all by myself. Watching television news and following online infection and death records scared me to the bone. The views of refrigerated truck-morgues in major hospitals grieved and scared me to death. Such views unfortunately brought me painful memories about my departed spouse. Even though I knew many of the media stories were scientifically unreal, I still experienced grave anxiety. I remember one day listening to Dr. Anthony Fauci (the famous US infectious disease specialist) in his discussion of statistical data that revealed the greater possibility of African-American people dying from coronavirus than any other racial group in the country.

Are people of color cursed or what? Is the conspiracy that the racist White population is seeking a way to eliminate the Black race becoming a reality? I questioned myself.

Dr. Fauci's data analysis was accurate. Still, it was painful for me as a person of color. On countless occasions, I asked depressing questions.

What if I terribly suffer from COVID-19 and die? What if I could not breathe in the night? What will happen if my children did not hear from me again? What if one of my children suffered COVID-19 and I could not be present? Suddenly the Spirit of God would jab me to pray in faith. Prayers helped tremendously. Still, there were times I felt mentally incapacitated to do groceries at Walmart. Even when I did, I exercised extreme caution never to touch a surface. I wore gloves. Still, I sanitized every fruit or vegetable I picked. Upon return, I would undress at my door, dump clothes in the washer, and bury myself under the shower. This was routine every day after work.

Chemistry is not an easy subject for the average college student. The Zoom lectures were not so bad, but teaching chemistry labs using kits and virtual platforms was terrible. The lab kits were not only expensive for students but they were too difficult and time-consuming to set up for the generation and analysis of chemical data. Some of the students had so much trouble that setting up the kits exhausted their lab hours. Some parents probably suffered greater anxiety than their wards. They had every reason to be; the cost of higher education is becoming increasingly astronomical. In one of my classes one day, I had no option but to politely call out a parent because of her unnecessary interference in her daughter's home classroom. Her biggest fear was that her daughter's struggle with online general chemistry was potentially going to ruin her ambition to go to medical school. In another case, I was forced to drive forty-five minutes to Murfreesboro to set up a lab kit for a student who got very depressed because of her inability to measure heat capacity using a calorimeter. The importance of distance and virtual learning has been widely discussed in pedagogical literature. Flipped classrooms, for instance, have become even more popular since the COVID-19 pandemic. A flipped classroom is where students consume instructional content (mostly videos) on their own at home and then use class time for discussion and activities. The flipped classroom model allows students to work at their own pace, and educators can use class time more creatively. The question is: Is it effective for every student? A review by Shivangi Dhawan in 2020 (*Journal Ed. Technol., 2020, 49 (1) 5–22*) has shown that many students missed out during the pandemic for many different reasons. First, students have varied learning styles, and some students learn much better under traditional, face-to-face conditions. Flipped classrooms, for instance, demand enormous self-discipline, which truly is a problem for many young people. Second, technology is expensive and not easily available for every family, even in an advanced country like the US. Third, not every academic discipline is amenable to virtual learning, particularly the natural sciences, where hands-on laboratory activities form a substantial part of pedagogy. Finally, the loss of the classroom learning community can be a disincentive, knowing that collaborative learning is a maturing space for young people in their future work environment.

The global population lost community engagements during the pandemic. I was no exception. I did not only miss my family but I missed my students as well. I missed my church family. Thankfully, Sunday services were livestreamed via Zoom. I learned to prepare my own Lord's Supper emblems and gave my financial contribution through online banking. The loss of social gatherings, including weddings, funerals, family vacations, was incalculable. One day, something very interesting happened. I received a church announcement from Brothers Kyle Duke and J. D. Blackburn inviting friends for a Sunday evening small group meeting. I jumped at that invitation. Like the tribe of Benjamin, I was surrounded by a large crowd of believers but still lacked a spiritual community. Words cannot express how J. D.'s friendship has blessed me ever since. We have studied the Bible together, had numerous conversations about life and spirituality, created a new circle of friends, enjoyed lake-fishing leisure, and simply enjoyed one another's company.

One day, one of our group members asked an important question: "What is the science behind the COVID-19 vaccines?" The following was my explanation adapted from an online publication by the American Academy of Pediatrics (May 2021).

Many Americans have been immunized at one time or another. In fact, many of our citizens continue to receive flu-vaccines to protect against new variants of the flu virus every year. The COVID-19 vaccine works similarly to all other vaccines. The SARS-CoV-2, which causes COVID-19, is known to invade and multiply inside the body cell. The vaccine stops this by teaching the immune system to recognize and making antibodies to fight the virus. After vaccination, we have less of a chance of getting COVID-19. And even if we get infected, we shall not be as sick as we would without the vaccine. Three different vaccines were given emergency use authorization by the U.S. Food and Drug Administration (FDA) so far. The Pfizer and Moderna vaccines require two doses, while the Johnson & Johnson vaccines requires a single dose. The distribution of the Johnson & Johnson vaccine was temporarily paused to look for possible ties to rare but serious blood clots reported during the vaccine's safety monitoring process. The FDA lifted the pause when the data confirmed that the chance of developing the clots with the vaccine was extremely low. However, they continue to monitor the risk factors. The Pfizer and Moderna two-dose vaccines are called messenger ribonucleic acid (mRNA) vaccines.

The Johnson & Johnson vaccine was developed as a "viral vector" vaccine. Fortunately, they all produce the same result. They both protect people from COVID-19, even though their delivery systems are a bit different. The Pfizer vaccine for example, does not contain any live or dead parts of the virus. Instead, it is made up of nucleic acids, which are the building blocks of all our cells. Once they have completed their job, they fall apart and exit the body.

The COVID-19 mRNA vaccines carry instructions to our cells to produce harmless pieces of "spike" protein found on SARS-CoV-2. This triggers an immune system response that the body remembers if the virus ever invades. Although this technology has been studied for decades, the widespread use of mRNA vaccines is new. As noted above, they do not use the live coronavirus that causes COVID-19. The mRNA in the vaccine gets into the cells where the shot is given. Then it gives the cells instructions on how to create a piece of protein that is found on the virus that causes COVID-19. Once the protein is created, the patient's immune system identifies it as a foreign molecule. Then, the immune process starts making antibodies that attach to the protein. These antibodies then protect the individual from getting COVID-19. The Johnson & Johnson viral vector vaccines, like the mRNA vaccines, also give instructions to a person's immune cells. Instead of carrying the instructions to our cells on a fat bubble, as with the mRNA vaccine, they are carried in a harmless virus (not the coronavirus that causes COVID-19). The same process happens as with the mRNA vaccine. The cells create the protein that is found on the virus that causes COVID-19, the immune system then makes antibodies to fight it, providing protection from COVID-19.

Although the COVID-19 vaccines are safe, both adults and adolescent children have reported certain short-term side effects. These include pain, redness, and swelling where the inoculation was given, fever, chills, headache, fatigue, nausea, and pain in the muscles. I personally experienced some of these side effects after the first and second doses of the Pfizer vaccine, which lasted a couple of days. But I know several people who never experienced any side effects at all. While some citizens reported side effects after their first dose, others experienced side effects after the second dose. God created everyone uniquely and differently!

12

Rules for Living

It was one of those hot evenings in October. The moon was shining bright. Many of my friends, both boys and girls, were busy playing in the street in front of our old estate house. My cousins were out to play too, but not me. I was too anxious to go out. My brain was burning like hot coal. But my anxiety was mixed with excitement because I was ready to move from home to start boarding secondary school the next day. I was scared about the unknown but excited because I had gained what I always wanted—high school education, which could potentially change my destiny forever. Already, I have been late for more than three weeks because of poverty. Now there was no more time to waste. My mother had arrived from the village to say goodbye. She was as anxious as I was. Some of the stories she had heard regarding difficult circumstances at many boarding schools in Ghana were horrifying. The poor hungry meals, bullying, bad youthful habits of smoking, drugs, and teenage sex were quite well-known. Besides, she was not sure whether I would pursue my Christian upbringing, continue as a chorister, or pursue my interest in piano. What was killing her the most was the length of the school year. Students in Ghanaian boarding schools followed a lengthy academic year with short breaks for Christmas and Easter. The most they spent with parents during my time was the long vacation from early July until the end of August. The chance to visit home was very rare unless one had special written permission called exeat.

My mother had some important advice before I left home for school. "Son, whosoever will shall prevail, but whosoever disregards counsel shall surely regret," she said.

"What does that mean, mother?" I asked.

"Only three things will make you successful. God-fearing boys grow to become successful men," she said. "Your school is a Methodist school, so Sunday church must remain your everyday life. Children who throw away God throw away life," she emphasized. Her mention of Sunday church reminisced the punishment I endured when I once skipped church to play soccer. That Sunday morning, I played soccer in place of church and went starving most part of the day as punishment.

Can that happen at the boarding school? Surely, not! I consoled myself.

Aside from God and church, my mother talked about self-control and respect for authority and school rules. "Because I will not be there to watch you do and how you do it, it is only self-control that will make you successful," she said. "You must learn to respect the little you have and stay away from affluent students who can potentially lead you into trouble," she added. "Even though we have never lived in plenty, we have also never lived a life of misery. Never forget that," she concluded.

The final thing my mother talked about was focusing on books. To her, I was the ugliest among her children. She and my sisters never stopped teasing me about my looks, which repeatedly annoyed me. On this occasion, however, she teased me about my looks to make a solid point. "Ugly guys like you must focus on school in order to succeed," she teased. "Consider your distant uncle, Lawyer Asiedu. He is not handsome, but look, education has taken him across the world," she stressed.

In my village, Lawyer Asiedu was the most revered and honored. When he was probably my age, he enrolled in one of the best boys' boarding high schools in the country, worked extremely hard, and earned Government of Ghana scholarship to pursue degrees in law and economics at Oxford University and the University of London. He returned home in the late 1970s during the hard economic days of Ghana's history. But because of his enormous professional capabilities, he was appointed legal counsel and later on, deputy chief executive officer of the Ghana Cocoa Board by the then-military government. He was a role model for every boy in my village. He was cousin to my mother. And she never ceased pronouncing how successful I would be if I ever studied as hard as Uncle Asiedu.

My mother's advice at age fifteen has ultimately anchored my rules for living. Professionally, I have lived and worked quite successfully outside my country of birth mainly because of godly fear, self-control, and love for learning. Stories upon stories validate this.

I have remained an ardent Bible student and scrutineer of the Holy Scriptures. Am I a perfect person? Never in this world! I have struggled with sin for years and continue to battle iniquity. My greatest check against misdeeds is my family. The wife of my youth remained my greatest admonisher and rebuker before she passed. In her place, my two daughters have assumed the role of close monitors. How I recovered from certain missteps can be attributed to their firm and harsh rebuke. The question is, Do I still fear God? Absolutely! Do I always know and understand what God wants for me? Not always. No humans are perfect, and if we were, we would not need a Savior. Many years ago, I had a wonderful opportunity to study the Bible with a Muslim friend called Konté. Konté did not consider himself the best Muslim. Still, he took his Islamic principles very seriously. Numerous times, we discussed religious instructions as inspired by the Koran or Bible. Konté had no real problems with Old Testament scripture. To him, its Pentateuch, history, poetry, and prophetic writings amply coincided with his understanding of the Holy Koran. His biggest criticism was against the writings of the New Testament. His problem was that Jesus Christ was portrayed as the Son of God and Savior of the world instead of a simple Jewish prophet. He was indignant when I confessed the atoning blood of Jesus for my sins. To him, history only portrayed Jesus Christ as a Jewish prophet assassinated by Roman soldiers because of his revolutionary religious and political views. He was dead and gone like all other ancient prophets.

"How could a human being save his fellow man from sin?" he questioned. "Would it not be wise for believers to directly pray to God for forgiveness of their sins than depending on another person? he queried.

This was my answer. "Never have I succeeded in a sinless life, no matter how hard I have tried. Not that I have not tried. I have tried countless times without success, and God is my witness. Because of such insufficiency did I decide Christ Jesus as my advocate, with his atoning blood as my refuge."

This is what the Bible says:

> In fact, according to the law of Moses, nearly everything was purified with blood. For without the shedding of blood, there is no forgiveness. (Hebrews 9:22)

The Hebrew writer pointedly confirms my point of view—"Jesus Christ is Lord and Savior."

> So Christ has now become the High Priest over all the good things that have come. He has entered that greater, more perfect Tabernacle in heaven, which was not made by human hands and is not part of this created world. With his own blood—not the blood of goats and calves—he entered the Most Holy Place once for all time and secured our redemption forever.
>
> Under the old system, the blood of goats and bulls and the ashes of a heifer could cleanse people's bodies from ceremonial impurity. Just think how much more the blood of Christ will purify our consciences from sinful deeds so that we can worship the living God. For by the power of the eternal Spirit, Christ offered himself to God as a

perfect sacrifice for our sins. That is why he is the
one who mediates a new covenant between God
and people, so that all who are called can receive
the eternal inheritance God has promised them.
For Christ died to set them free from the penalty
of the sins they had committed under that first
covenant. (Hebrews 9:11–16 NLT)

Am I the only beneficiary as a Bible student? The answer is no.
Many believers have reaped golden values from the Holy Scriptures.
Years ago, I asked how a trusted friend became that successful as an
African executive. A continent where genuine businesspersons are as
rare as tanzanite. His answer was simple: "The Bible taught me how
to do genuine and profitable business." I can identify with his view-
point. How I wish my mother were here. How proud would she have
been to see how God has transformed and extended my influence
for human good? Over the past three decades, I have served many
church leadership roles—Bible class teacher, deacon, preacher, elder,
and missionary. All to the glory of God!

Ghana is a peaceful country with a low crime rate. Nevertheless,
where I grew up in Kumasi was notorious for gang crimes, drugs,
and teenage sex. My mother's advice on self-control saved me from
trouble. Several teenage girls I grew up with quit school because boys
or older men impregnated them. Teenage parents perpetuated their
own parents' cycle of poverty. One of my half-brothers was murdered
because of his affair with the killer's wife. My second half-brother died
because of drug addiction. Protection from my mother was immense,
but the fact is that instructions from church ministers and Bible
teachers accentuated my understanding and practice of self-control.
What church did extra was a diligent reinforcement of my mother's
protection. Yet I remember a few brushes with youthful sexual exper-
imentation, which produced disastrous consequences. Fortunately,
I escaped disintegration. What those bad experiences created was a
forceful resistance to peer pressure, alcohol, and drug use. Not once,
not twice, but on numerous occasions, some of my friends ridiculed
my love for church and lack of entertainment. Hardly did they realize

that church was actually more fun for me than they thought. Our youth group was quite well organized and better placed than the brawling parties my friends were associated with.

Aside from gospel campaigns and engaging biblical studies, we played games, enjoyed meal fellowships, traveled on excursions, and enjoyed hanging out during vacations. The bonds we formed led to solid acquaintances and subsequently, healthy marriages. Evelyn and I were a typical example. Our Christian convictions and friendships were stronger than the average tweens in our neighborhood. Evelyn once told me a story. She and I were insanely deprived. Yet we deeply loved and cared about each other during our college days. Many members of our local church also recognized our devotion to one another. According to her, one of the richest church families secretly schemed by giving her generous gifts with the aim of snatching her for their son. They did this with the intention of taking advantage of her economic deficit. When she finally realized their plot, she immediately returned all their gifts. This is one proof that want and poverty were not enough to erode our self-control as young believers.

My mother's advice on priority education was spot-on. There is no doubt this has done me a ton of good now. Not in one's wildest dreams would anyone who knew my childhood imagine I would ever become a scientist or an academic in the US. At both high school and college, I tried to work harder than my peers did. I succeeded not because I was the best student but because I learned to be determined. I learned one important lesson about this while in high school. It was rumored that our headmaster (Mr. P.) gave Mr. S. a job as the senior housemaster not because of the latter's competence but purely out of the former's compassion. We found out that both were very close friends during their teacher training college years. While Mr. P. broke his back completing schoolwork, Mr. S. idled and played board games most of the time. Ultimately, they both graduated, with Mr. P. obtaining much better grades compared to his companion. Mr. P. proceeded to earn two graduate degrees in education from the University of Ghana and subsequently developed a highly successful career in high school administration. One day, someone knocked at his office door looking for a job as a history teacher. This was Mr. S., but they both failed to recognize each other. Several years had elapsed since they left their previous college. Besides, age had caught up with them. But when they finally reconnected to their past, Mr. P. was utterly surprised how frail his old friend had become. On the other hand, Mr. S. was amazed how agile and impeccable his former friend was looking. There was no open position for history except vernacular. Mr. P. felt pity and offered his old friend the job before personally sponsoring his retraining. Over time, Mr. S. was appointed the senior housemaster but often displayed low self-confidence in the presence of the headmaster. I have not ceased using this story in educating young people about the value of focusing on school. The search for knowledge can be painfully slow and exhausting, but there is no question about the rewards therefrom.

13

Why Take Things for Granted?

"What organized chaos," said Harry.

"What incredible poverty," noted Stephanie.

"Kids at Kojokrom are unbelievably poor. I might not survive a week here," said Drew. These were some of the few comments I recorded from some of my American students who joined me on a mission and a study-abroad trip to Ghana about a decade ago. For a couple of them, Ghana was not only their first travel abroad but also air travel out of state. Since then, more than thirty American students have joined my mission trips to Africa.

The road journey to Kojokrom was very exciting. We arrived at the Accra International Airport sometime in late July 2012. The weather was warm and humid. July is typically wet. There are only two marked seasons in West Africa—the wet and dry seasons. The wet season is influenced by southwest monsoons, which drive heavy thunderstorms and rainfall across the Gulf of Guinea. The mornings and evenings were breezy and cool, but the afternoons were sticky hot in coastal Accra. We toured a few interesting places. We visited the gorgeous royal-designed presidential palace, arts and science museum, W. E. B. DuBois Center and the bustling Makola market. The next morning, we drove more than two hundred miles to Kojokrom en route to the suffocating N1 highway. The N1 highway is also called the George W. Bush Highway in honor of the former US president whose institution of the Millennium Challenge Corporation follow-ing a 2004 act of the US Congress provided financial aid for building the highway. The road was long and exhausting. Because of narrow and terrible road networks, traveling a short distance in Africa can be more strenuous than trekking the Himalayas. Hardly are there any rest areas, eateries, gas stations, or restrooms. Evelyn had the hardest task of teaching our American female students how to use the nearby bush as a restroom. "In Africa, everywhere is a restroom," said one student. How sad! Today, however, one can find a few gas stations with makeshift restrooms. Ten years ago, that was impossible.

We checked into a small hotel and treated ourselves to the leg-endary Ghanaian jollof rice with chicken when we finally arrived. After a brief devotional, we retired to bed, fatigued. Our mission plan was simple—house-to-house preaching, Bible seminars, and visit to the countryside. Day after day, we trekked the surrounding villages proclaiming the gospel of Jesus Christ. Ghanaians are some of the friendliest people in the world. Although poor, their openness and sense of hospitality are unrivaled. They shared history and stories about their villages and pampered us with delicious tropical fruits including fresh mangoes, coconuts, oranges, and pineapples. In most parts of West Africa, foods typically are fresh, organically cultivated, tree-ripened, and yummy.

Wherever we went, several children followed us with excitement, like biblical times. The children were just adorable. Seeing foreigners, they came shouting: "Obroni, obroni" meaning "White man, White man." The very smart ones distinguished the Africans from the Americans judging by their respective English accents. While taking a break at the village square one steamy afternoon, Harry, an African American missionary, attempted to explain to some boys why he was not "obroni" (White man) but simply fair in complexion.

"I am not 'obroni.' I am 'obibini' (i.e., Black man)," said Harry. "Look at the color of my skin. It is black like yours," he told them.

One little boy looked at Harry's face closely, examined his skin and palm, and exclaimed, "No way, sir! You are definitely 'obroni.' You speak like an American. You are not like this man," he said, pointing at me. "Look at him, he is not 'obroni.' He is from Ghana.

He speaks like a Ghanaian." We were cracking up. To them, "obroni" meant more than skin color. They had no idea that certain Black people are born US citizens. In their village, all they understood was that every Black person lived in Ghana and all Americans were White. Poor boys!

While some sub-Saharan African countries like Ghana, Nigeria, Ivory Coast, Kenya, Angola, Botswana, Rwanda, and Tanzania have witnessed remarkable improvements in their national economies the past three decades, much of the continent is still very poor. The situation in rural areas is brazenly acute. In Ghana, rural children still swim across rivers before attending school. Years ago, I remember traveling to a village in the Savannah Region of Ghana where only one teacher was responsible for an entire elementary school. His classroom was under a large tree, with his blackboard nailed to the trunk. The students brought their own wooden stools and copied scripted notes with notebooks on their laps. Several countries do not provide lunch for schoolchildren, and people have no access to proper shelter, clean water, toilet, and electricity. Even in large towns, some children graduate from schools without any ability to read or write. According to Jennifer O'Neill of Global Citizen (2016),

> access to quality schools is hardest felt in Sub-Saharan Africa. Nine out of ten countries with the highest percentages of children who have never attended school were in Africa during the 2000s. And today, the ten lowest-ranked countries in the United Nations' Human Development Report Education Index are in Africa. And while recent years have seen a rise in school enrollment, serious challenges still face poverty-plagued countries grappling with how to provide access to education, keep kids in school, and foster learning. The picture that these numbers paint is not pretty, but as the stories of these countries show, there is always some hope.

This is hardly the case in the US. Most American children have access to good education, school bus, and lunch. Despite complaints against inner-city education, facilities are still far superior to most parts of Africa, Southeast Asia, and South America. While tuition for high schools is completely free in the US, less than 30 percent of young Africans receive free tuition in high school. In Europe, eight countries (e.g., Scandinavian countries, Germany, Greece, Austria, and France) provide free education for their citizens even up to the university level. In Africa, this only partially happens in countries like Egypt, Morocco, and Kenya.

What the American youth cannot take for granted is their personal freedoms, religious liberty, and democratic governance. America is truly blessed with a highly diverse hardworking population, colossal economy, excellent educational and medical facilities, and enormous opportunities for personal development. Why the American youth has no reason not to develop themselves is well described by blogger R. J. Wilson (2017). America is enormously affluent, and here are some reasons.

America has a reliable infrastructure

One of the things the American youth take for granted is physical infrastructure. It is important to know that most of the time, a bridge will not collapse, and one can be confident that their toilet will flush whenever they need it. Not only that but there are also so many countries where housing is nonexistent, there is no clean potable water, electricity, or asphalted roads to travel. According to the World Economic Forum, the United States is ranked eleventh among countries by infrastructure score, which is behind other developed countries like the United Kingdom, Germany, Japan, but certainly one of the best globally. There is little doubt that the US needs to upgrade its physical infrastructure including schools, hospitals, roads, and airports; but thankfully, the country is in a good position to do so, especially now that an infrastructure investment policy has drawn bipartisan support in Congress.

Gasoline is cheap

Politics and economics are the two most important reasons why gasoline is relatively cheap in the US. The fact remains that gasoline is far cheaper than most parts of the world. Currently, the average cost of gasoline in the US is about $2.85 per gallon while it is $7.12 in Hong Kong, $6.02 in the United Kingdom, $5.38 in Germany, and $7.04 in Norway. Since 1993, gas taxes have never been increased, which ensures economic benefit to all the American people.

Food and meat are cheap

Globally, food prices have significantly increased over the past three decades. However, food prices have remained relatively stable in the US. According to the U.S. Department of Agriculture (USDA), the average food consumption per consumer per year in 2012 was about $2,273, representing nearly 6.4 percent of average income. When the USDA compared this data with 83 countries, US consumers were found to spend a much smaller percentage on food than all those countries. Some economists think this question is debatable since it is easy for American incomes to go significantly farther in many of the countries studied. In India, for instance, one can easily buy a gallon of milk for less than a dollar. By economic theory, one could argue that Americans pay more than we think since part of our annual tax bill goes toward farm subsidies. Still, even after adjusting for subsidies, food in the United States is relatively cheaper. What is more American than a nice, juicy steak? Meat consumption in the United States stands at an incredible 270.7 pounds per person per year. That is more than any other country on the planet except for Luxembourg (tiny city-country in Europe). Research shows that Americans now eat more chicken than beef. In fact, chicken passed beef as the nation's favorite meat in 2010. Because of healthy eating, many more Americans are now eating more turkey, which is still greater than much of the Western world.

Life expectancy is high

According to the WHO, the average life expectancy of American citizens is about 79.3 years, which ranks thirty-first on the global scale. Japan has the highest average life expectancy of about 83.7 years. While America's longevity is relatively lower compared to other Western countries, it is still enormous globally. In other places like Sierra Leone and Cuba, the average life expectancy is about 50 years. The good part is that America has some of the best medical care, and many of the causes of premature deaths are preventable according to the US Centers for Disease Control and Prevention (CDC). The CDC has reported that in the past decade, fewer Americans died from preventable causes, meaning American citizens are getting healthier and making better health decisions overall.

There is plenty of room

The United States has a population density of 85.53 people per square mile. Globally, that puts us at 182nd among countries and territories. By comparison, the population density of Monaco is an incredible 49,236 people per square mile. In densely populated countries, pollution is a bigger issue, and people often live in tiny, cramped spaces in massive apartment buildings. Overcrowding can cause serious humanitarian issues, and even when buildings are carefully planned, high population densities can make for a stressful existence. That is generally not an issue for Americans. Of course, there are a few disadvantages to having all that room. If one lived in a rural part of the United States, one will almost certainly need an automobile to get around, whereas owning a car would actually be a liability in other parts of the world.

Government is "less corrupt"

It is common knowledge that members of US Congress roll around in giant money pits before signing papers lobbyists put in front of them. It is true that the American democracy has big issues.

Still, Corruption Perception Index reports rank the US government on a score of sixty-nine, indicating a "less corrupt" government compared to a global average. This ranks US twenty-third on a global scale behind countries like the Netherlands, Canada, Germany, and Sweden, but ahead of countries like Ireland, Japan, Chile, and Poland. According to this index, the country with the least amount of corruption is Denmark, with an outstanding score of 90. But given the size and age of the United States, government corruption does not appear to unnecessarily impact the socioeconomic conditions of its citizens.

America has the largest economy

Without a doubt, China's economy is a tremendous boost. Nevertheless, the United States still superintends the world's largest economy, with a gross domestic product (GDP) of about $18.56 trillion. To put this in perspective, the entire European Union possesses a GDP of $17.11 trillion while China's GDP is estimated at $11.39 trillion. The next richest country is Japan, with a GDP of about $4.7 trillion. Despite the effects of COVID-19, the US continues to benefit from moderate unemployment, a high average annual salary, and a business-friendly economic climate, which gives hope for even a much brighter future.

Why at all is America's economic data relevant? Without a doubt, every place on our planet has unique characteristics, Africa inclusive. Ghana is an exceptionally friendly and beautiful country. One must visit to experience her people, culture, food, tropical landscapes, unspoiled beaches, and safaris. Even crocodiles are friendly, and this is no exaggeration! American students have had the chance to walk lofty canopy walks on Amazon-like tropical trees and petted gigantic tropical crocodiles in national parks. One only pays a pittance to have such a lifetime experience. Nevertheless, the level of poverty is inestimable. The scarcity of good roads and jobs is a major headache, even for national security. At the same time, many African political leaders are so greedy and corrupt that the cultivation of a sustained social and economic discipline is as difficult as growing wings. Therefore, the youth in the Western world must never take opportunities in their countries for granted. The grace of God and the toils of their ancestors must never be trivialized. In other words, the freedoms in America must not be undervalued, and the seemingly endless possibilities for a better life must never be considered inconsequential.

The harsh poverty and stresses I constantly faced while growing up have taught me two very important lessons—never to take anything for granted, and continue to lean on the ever-present, providential arms of God. There is nothing I have achieved or can do today that was not handed to me by grace. I have tried to teach my own family this and pray they stick to it. And I hope America and the world are listening.

14

Transcended

Transcended, how transcended! How I wish my mother were still here to see how my life has transcended beyond expectation. She had no idea how her poor son would influence humanity, except perhaps only through her impeccable lens of faith. Who in the world would have thought that an African village boy born into a disastrous polygamous family and raised in inner-city slums would become a chemistry professor in three different universities in Africa, Great Britain, and the US? My mother was uneducated. How she most accurately predicted that godly fear, education, and self-control would lift me from poverty still blows my mind.

Now I know she was not alone. No teacher better inspired my education when growing up than my eighth-grade teacher called Mr. Daniel. His full name was Mr. Daniel Soadzedey, but for the fear of mispronouncing his last name and courting displeasure, we all called him Mr. Daniel. That was easier. He was the one who paid my common entrance examination registration fees which passaged my admittance to high school. He was also the teacher who privately tutored me to ace the regional high school admissions test. Still, he was the one who bugged my mother to prioritize my education. I have forgotten many of his wise sayings; however, one of his best maxims has stuck with me. He preached excellence like it were a biblical sermon.

Persistently, he made the following statement:

> Aim high, so that when you fall, you fall
> on treetops. But don't aim at treetops because
> when you fall, you may fall below the level of the
> ground.

Mr. Daniel's words were strong and unequivocal. He preached "excellence" almost daily in his class. He was himself a self-achiever. Like many of his students, he was raised from a very poor family but self-educated until he graduated from a poorly paid teacher into one of Ghana's topmost insurance executives. Unfortunately, because of alcoholism and mental illness, his otherwise illustrious life was terminated abruptly. Nothing else has shaped my conduct and professionalism than the hunger for spirituality, studiousness, self-control, and excellence. I have always pushed for distinction not only in academia but also in family, religious, and social life. Have I been super successful? The answer is no. I have faced and continue to face many serious challenges. But have I given every situation my best shot? Absolutely! I have always tried to put my best foot forward in many different circumstances and conditions—at home, local community, church, and workplace.

As an academic, I have witnessed public recognition of several colleagues because of their excellent professional service. In many instances, I have seized the opportunity to shout for them with admiration and positive envy. "How I wish I would be recognized as the best chemistry professor one day?" I spoke quietly to myself. The fact is, no student evaluation of a chemistry professor is excellent. Many students of chemistry think their instructors are just mean. They only forget that the subject is simply hard. Something happened before the start of the 2021 fall semester. Back from COVID-19 lockdowns, we returned to one of our annual academic rituals at an in-person faculty and staff workshop. Meetings like that are important for recharging our batteries to welcome new and continuing students for the start of the school year. This particular workshop was designed to allow the dean of the College of Liberal Arts and Sciences (Dr. David

Holmes) to rearticulate his vision to his staff. Nearly two hundred of my colleagues were present. Speaker upon speaker shared their thoughts, led devotionals, and spoke words of wisdom and encouragement. Finally, it was the turn of Dean Holmes. David is a gifted speaker but can sometimes be unpredictable. As one of the departmental chairs, I was assigned a front-row seat in the roomy Ward Lecture Hall at the Lipscomb McFarland Science Center. Before his address, David beckoned me to stand up. I felt quite uncomfortable. *Did I do something wrong?* I kept musing in my head. He tried to explain the essence of my invitation. His final comment was that he considered me as one of his hardworking departmental leaders. He further announced that out of a dozen or so strategic plans he reviewed from departments under his oversight, my report was the best-articulated and most comprehensive. The applause for me was profound and deafening. I was proud but emotional. Although the recognition was not the type that comes with colorful certification or orated citation, I could still not be prouder. This was unexpected, but the very recognition by colleagues was just overwhelming. I learned one more lesson that day. Whatever act of kindness or excellence, however minuscule, will never go unrewarded.

Elsewhere, I expressed my greatest love for the leaders and members of the Grand Central Church of Christ (GC) in West Virginia. Their faith and love for kingdom work are incomparable. My family is always blessed whenever we go back to visit. One summer weekend, we returned to GC for church service. The welcome was expectedly heartwarming. When we were members there a few years ago, I tried to create an enduring love for congregational prayers. My approach was to pronounce priestly blessings upon worshippers at the conclusion of every church service, drawing several biblical quotes and examples. My most favorite quote was the Aaronic pastoral benediction from Numbers 6:24–26 (NIV).

> The LORD said to Moses, "Tell Aaron and his sons, 'This is how you are to bless the Israelites. Say to them: The LORD bless you and keep you; the LORD make his face shine on you

and be gracious to you; the LORD turn his face
toward you and give you peace.'"

What a legacy. I had no idea how this will ever be. In fact,
I never knew how my simple everyday benediction would inspire
some of God's people in America. The elders invited me to bless the
congregation. After the church service, I watched the lovely faces of
worshippers who thronged to greet me—men, women, and children.
They were filled with immense joy. Tears rolled down the cheeks of
some of my best friends. "Your legacy of priestly blessings is now a
Sunday routine," said one of the elders. "Your light and influence
have never and will never dim here," he concluded. If this is not a life
transformed beyond reason, what else is?

The foregoing narration will be incomplete without one or two
brief classroom stories. Just like we found it uncomplimentary to
mispronounce our teacher's last name years ago, I have frequently
noticed the difficulty some of my American friends and students face
in trying to respect my African double-barrel last name. Don't we
all once in a while face problems like that? We most certainly do!
Modern civilization has truly blessed native English speakers in dis-
seminating their language across the globe. The downside, however,
is that it is as hard as a rock for English speakers to learn a new language. My students are no exception. One day, one of my students
(now a physician) decided to simplify the process by branding me
as Dr. OD. I never disavowed him, and this has remained my name
across campus ever since. For many students, my name is not what
is important but my passion for teaching science and the ease with
which I get them excited about chemistry. Has this clearly reflected
my student evaluations? I would say no. Still, that has not prevented
a good number of students from appreciating my genuine proclivity
in support of their education. One of them is young Diyari. When
I first met her in my summer organic chemistry class, Diyari shared
her ambition to pursue a medical career after college. She was clearly
one of the sweetest students any professor would welcome in their
class. Her intellectual ability and desire for excellence was plainly
visible. My experience as an educator is that inquisitive and diligent

learners are those who never fail to excel. Diyari portrayed such attitude adorably. When the course concluded, a letter of appreciation came through the mail from her (see attached). Like the alabaster perfume woman in Mark 14:1–9, Diyari merits a mention in these concluding pages, and my influence on students like her is the reason why this book is worth your time.

Dear Dr. OD,

Thank you for such an amazing semester and for making organic chemistry much more exciting and fun for us than ever. I am forever grateful and am sending prayers your way as you embark on your missionary trip. The way you will bring God into many of their lives in Africa is beautiful and I can't wait to come visit you in the fall and ask all about how it went. I was also hoping that when the time comes in the fall, you'd give me the honor of having one of my medschool recommendation letters from you. I am beyond thankful for this experience in your class and wish for a safe and successful missionary trip.

Best regards,
Diyari Bekhtyar

REFERENCES

Adu-Boahen, Albert. 2000. *Ghana: Evolution and Change in the Nineteenth and Twentieth Centuries.* Sankofa Educational Publications Ltd.

Adu-Gyamfi, Samuel, Wilhemina J. Donkor, and Anim Adinkra Addo. 2017. "Educational Reforms in Ghana: Past and Present." *Journal of Education and Human Development,* 5(3), pp. 158–172.

Akyeampong, Kwame. 2010. "Educational Expansion and Access in Ghana: A Review of 50 years of Challenge and Progress." *Research Monograph No. 33.*

American Association of Pediatrics. 2022. "COVID-19 Vaccines in Children and Adolescents." *Pediatrics,* p. 149, e2021054332: https://doi.org/10.1542/peds.2021-054332.

Antwi, Moses K. 1992. *Education: Society and Development in Ghana.* Unimax Publishers Ltd.

Calisher, Charles H., Dennis Carroll, Rita Colwell, Ronald B Corley, Peter Daszak, et al. 2021. "Science, not speculation, is essential to determine how SARS-CoV-2 reached humans." *The Lancet.* https://doi.org/10.1016/S0140-6736(21)01419-7, published online July 5, 2021.

De Jong, Gerald Francis. 2009. *The Dutch Reformed Church and Negro Slavery in Colonial America.* Cambridge Press, pp. 423–436.

Dhawan, S. 2020. "Online Learning: A Panacea in the Time of COVID-19 Crisis." *Journal of Educational Technology Systems,* doi:10.1177/0047239520934018.

Hartog, Paul. 2014. "The Maltreatment of Early Christians: Refinement and Response." *Southern Baptist Journal of Theology*, 18.1, pp. 49–79.

Morens, David M. and Anthony S. Fauci. 2012. "Emerging Infectious Diseases in 2012: 20 Years after the Institute of Medicine Report." *AMS Journals*, mBio, vol. 3, issue 6, e00494-12: https//doi.org/10.1128/mBio.00494.12.

O'Neill, Jennifer. 2016. "The World's 10 Worst Countries for Education Are in Africa." Global Citizen's *Defeat Poverty* online publication series.

Opoku-Duah, Stephen. 2013. "Vegetation and Drought Mapping in West Africa Using Remote Sensing: A Case Study." *Online Journal of Social Sciences Research*, 2(6), pp. 142–150.

Pew Research Center. 2019. "In US, Decline of Christianity Continues at Rapid Pace: An Update on America's Changing Religious Landscape."

Pokhrel, Sumitra and Roshan Chhetri. 2021. "A Literature Review on Impact of COVID-19 Pandemic on Teaching and Learning." *Higher Education for the Future*, https://doi.org/10.1177/2347631120983481.

Wilson, R. J. 2017. "Eight Things Americans Take for Granted (But Shouldn't)."

Websites

Center for Disease Control and Prevention (CDC): https://www.cdc.gov/vaccines/schedules/hcpl/imz/child-adolescent.html.

Durham University: https://www.durham.ac.uk/homepage.

Hu Xijin: https://www.globaltimes.cn/author/Hu-Xijin.html.

Johns Hopkins COVID-19 Tracking Resource Center: www.coronavirus.jhu.edu.

Kwame Nkrumah University of Science and Technology: https://www.knust.edu.gh.

Lipscomb University: https://www.lipscomb.edu.

New York Post: https://nypost.com/2021/03/26/fauci-refutes-ex-cdc-directors-claim-that-covid-came-from-lab.

NIH—National Institute of Allergies and Infectious Diseases (NIAID): https://www.niaid.nih.gov/diseases-conditions/coronaviruses.

Ohio Valley University: https://www.ovu.edu.

United Nations Development Program (UNDP): www.hdr.undp.org.

United Nations—IOM/OECD: https://www.un.org/sites/un2.un.org/files/wmr_2020.pdf (World Migration Report: 2020).

Wageningen University and Research: https://www.wur.nl/en.htm.

World Health Organization (WHO): https://www.who.int/emergencies/diseases/novel-coronavirus-2019/situation-reports; https://www.who.int/data/gho/data/themes/topics/topic-details/GHO/healthy-life-expectancy-(hale).

Transparency International: https://www.transparency.org/en/about (Global Corruption Index: 2020 reports).

ABOUT THE AUTHOR

 Dr. Steve Opoku-Duah earned his doctorate degree in environmental hydrology from Durham University in England. For more than twenty years, he has taught graduate and undergraduate courses in chemistry and hydrology in three different countries. He has published widely in high-impact scientific journals, earned several academic and research awards, and served as a Christian missionary in Africa, Europe, and North America.

CPSIA information can be obtained
at www.ICGtesting.com
Printed in the USA
JSHW030913280223
38294JS00001B/4